How to help your child succeed at school

Dr Dominic Wyse

Consultancy and contributions by James Harrison

Author's note: I have elected to refer to a child alternately as 'he' or 'she' from
chapter to chapter to avoid the rather clumsy 'him/her', 'his/her' and 'he/she' options.

Pearson Education Limited
Edinburgh Gate
Harlow
Essex CM20 2JE
England

ISBN 978-0-273-71403-3

Commissioning Editor: Emma Shackleton
Project Editor: Helena Caldon
Designer: Annette Peppis
Cover illustration: Chris Long
Senior Production Controller: Man Fai Lau

Printed and bound in Spain by Graficas Estella

The Publisher's policy is to use paper manufactured from sustainable forests.

contents

Acknowledgements

With particular thanks to James Harrison for his work and support in the writing of this book.

I am also grateful to Emma Shackleton for the initial inspiration, and to Helena Caldon, Jeanette Payne and Annette Peppis for their work on the project. Last, but not least, my thanks to Stephanie Thwaites for her dedicated work at the earliest stage of the project.

This book is dedicated to my Mum, who said 'reach for the clouds and you'll hit the treetops'.

Introduction

Every parent wants something quite simple and fundamental from our education system: we want it to encourage our children to learn and also to give them the opportunities they need which will help them to be successful later in life – in whatever career or life path they choose to follow. It is probably fair to say that if this is your attitude, you are not alone: the vast majority of people in society want the same thing. For some people education is key because it dictates how culture is passed from one generation to the next; for others, such as those in business, it is important because it produces employees with strong skills; while politicians tell us that there are proven links between the quality of education and a nation's prosperity.

So, faced with the fact that there is pretty much universal agreement that education and learning is important – how can we help our children to make the most of the learning they are given and give them the support they need to realize their potential? This book aims to answer this question and leave you equipped and confident in helping your child succeed at school.

The ideas behind *How to Help Your Child Succeed at School* stem from the opinion that parents can better assist their children's learning if they have some knowledge about how the education system in this country works. A little knowledge can go a long way, but a lot of knowledge can go even further. So we begin by offering a set of basic principles that will guide you through the challenges that your child will face on his journey from nursery to university. The most important of these is the idea that learning starts from the day that your child is born and that learning does not just take place at school, it is a lifelong process. Another principle behind the book is that we are all teachers – yes, professional teachers have important skills that are different from those employed by most parents but, nevertheless, parents are responsible for teaching their children so many things. In fact, good teachers will acknowledge how much parents have to offer, too.

The goal of this book is an ambitious one. We aim to give you information about your child and his or her education from birth to age 18. As far as we know, there isn't another book like this that is specifically designed to help parents.

Once we have shared the basic principles with you, we won't just launch straight into your child's first school; in fact, we give you a little bit of homework to do – sorry! Before your child goes to his first playgroup or nursery you need to ask yourself a few questions, one of the most important being: how will you know whether the setting that your child could go to is good enough? In fact, this question is an important one for all the stages covered in the book: early years; primary school; secondary school; sixth form and university; and so we will direct you to the kind of information you can rely on to help you know which educational settings are high quality, while steering you away from less reliable sources at the same time! In order to help you make the decision as to which educational setting is best for your child, we will help you to find answers to key questions, such as: what do all these league tables mean and can we trust them? How useful is the playground gossip? What should you be looking out for when you visit a school or other setting? How much homework should your child get? And many other equally important issues, too.

The first education stage you will encounter is that of the early years – birth to age five – and what a fascinating and complex world this is! Once upon a time, education for children at this age was patchy, to say the least. Since then there has been an explosion of provision for young children, including voluntary, government-funded and private. Where once there was only two hours per day of education for your child at this young age (if you were lucky), in some places you can now get wrap-around care and education; so here we will sift through all the options and explain 10 different sorts of such early years provision. Do you know what the EYFS is? No? Well you'll find out in this first chapter.

The settings of primary and secondary schools are rather more straightforward, though. Legally, you have to send your child to school from the age of five years old, so the state has to provide places for children to be schooled. It is in primary school that you and your child will encounter the National Curriculum for the first time: this is the curriculum that teachers must deliver to your child. By law, your child will also sit their first 'SATs' at this age (see page 52); but don't panic, it doesn't have to be painful! Chapter 2 offers lots of information to help you and your child understand just how important the different assessments are; when they happen; and what their implications are for future learning. (I would also remind you, here and in Chapter 2, that as a voting member of the population you can have some influence over the fact that children in England are probably tested more than in any other country in the world. Ask yourself if the testing and target-setting system is really benefiting your child. If the answer to this is no, then you are perfectly within your rights to challenge the situation through practical political action, such as emailing your MP. Talking to other parents about this kind of issue can also be useful, particularly if it leads to political action and, hopefully, changes for the better.)

After the early years your child will go on to primary school. Although most primary schools group children together according to their achievements in maths and English, it is at secondary school that 'subject sets' become even more common. Again, we will explain what they are, the ways in which they are decided and, more importantly, how you can take an active part in decisions like these that are made about your child. An important section in the secondary school chapter is, of course, about how to choose GCSEs; these choices are also important because they will affect the subjects studied between the age of 16 and 18.

The final chapter of the book goes into this stage of education in more depth – focusing on age 16 and beyond. There are important decisions to be made about A levels and other qualifications at this stage, particularly if your child is planning to go on to university after school. We hope to take away some of the anxiety and help you to make the most informed decision that is appropriate for your child and their skills and ambitions. One of the most important issues at this stage is the difference between vocational and 'academic' education. Our view is that both of these are important, but it depends on your child's interests and strengths as to which route he will take. A key message here, and for the book as a whole, is about motivation. What is your child interested in? Has he got a passion for what he wants to do next? Can you help him find that passion?

Education has been my personal passion for a long time: it is in my blood. My mother was an early years teacher and still works training teachers; my father was a secondary teacher and still works with schools, helping them develop more exciting teaching and learning; my wife works for the school governor service in Cambridgeshire. I myself taught in primary schools in London, Bradford and Huddersfield before going into teacher-training in Liverpool, then finally moving to the University of Cambridge Faculty of Education, where I am involved in research and teaching and specializing in primary and early years education. And last, but certainly not least, my children are in the education system at the moment – aged 11 and 13.

As I wrote this introduction, yet another government education initiative had just been announced: a new curriculum for secondary schools which would retain the best of traditional teaching, but would also bring in much needed flexibility for pupils and teachers – giving them more influence over what they learn and teach. In the inspiring setting of Lord's Cricket Ground and in a fanfare of publicity, the new curriculum was announced. I was fortunate to be invited to this event. It was an occasion that turned out to be particularly memorable; in part because of the showcase of secondary pupils' music and art work, but also because it was high time that these kinds of changes were made to the curriculum.

However, a few weeks earlier, and with much less publicity, another government publication had been released called Every Parent Matters. The Education Minister said the initiative marked 'the beginning of what I hope will be a national debate with parents, children and young people, as well as service planners, commissioners and providers as to how parents can best be supported and engaged'. This is indeed good news, because it underlines how important parents are in the education of their children.

We hope that this book might make a small contribution to this educational debate; but although a national debate could be helpful in the long term, there is still much that you as a parent need to know now in order to help your child.

In the course of our book we take you on a journey from the nursery to the sixth form – but we don't want to stop there! The final section advises you how you can help your child to select a suitable university course while also assessing the pros and cons of newspaper university league tables. If that education stage is not relevant to your child, don't close the book there, because the final pages list important websites and books for parents of children of all ages, and these resources will give you essential information for all the phases of education this book has covered.

Once you have read this book we hope that you will feel even more confident to help your child through the exciting world of learning and education. Education is something that should be celebrated and treasured, because it is about your child's future and the future of all our children.

grasping
the basics

Everyone has an interest in education, because it touches all our lives. We all experience education by going to school; some then experience it at university, too. The world of work and its training can also be seen as an education. Some people talk of a 'university of life'! Having been through education ourselves we then help our children.

'Education, education, education' – with those three words the former Prime Minister, Tony Blair, summed up the vital importance of education to the nation. The other three words that are vital for you and your child are: 'learning, learning, learning'.

Life-long learning

The idea of 'life-long learning' is a fashionable one; but what does it mean for you and your child?

Essentially it means learning starts from birth. You talk to your child long before they can talk themselves; you play games with them (such as bouncing them on your knee); you use toys and other things to encourage their exploration of their world, and you are fascinated by their development (such as the first time they can sit up without support). So learning starts from birth. But it can also go on throughout life. Think of those people who retire then study for a degree. What about night classes in languages, pottery or sports? What about work training courses? And so it goes on.

We are all natural teachers

Not only are we all interested in learning but most of us are teachers, too; if you ever have to help someone to learn something you are effectively acting as a teacher. Nearly every occupation involves some form of teaching: the mechanic helping his friend mend a car, the squash player informally coaching a fellow player, a director discussing a scene with an actor, the choirmaster leading a choir and, of course, you, the parents, will also help your child to learn throughout his life.

One of the most important things to remember, though, is that if at a particular point in time your child struggles with learning (which, let's face it, most of us do), then you shouldn't worry unduly. Instead, focus on trying to understand the nature of the challenge, on giving your child the support he needs and on remaining positive. As this book will hopefully demonstrate to you, there are many educational phases you will need to face throughout your child's journey in learning.

Education: a step-by-step process...

Getting the best for your child at school is like hopping stepping stones over a stream. Nursery hops to reception class, then primary school, secondary school (or maybe middle school), university and/or careers advice. On the way there are also statutory tests (often known as SATs), GCSEs, AS levels, A levels and degrees.

Each of these places is a stone on which you must land in order to help your child progress across the stream. No two stones are the same, and while the next stone is obviously uppermost in your mind, you should also try to anticipate the stones ahead: their shape and size for landing on, distance apart, evenness, and so on. Each leap from stone to stone builds into a continual crossing, gaining knowledge and experience from the previous leap to better prepare you for the next stepping stone – and setting you up for the successful journey to the other side. This journey is as much a learning process for you as for your child.

The stages of education are shown in the table on page 16. In the left column is the age of the child, next to the National Curriculum Key Stages, which we will discuss later. The two right columns show the school years when statutory assessments are sat.

The long view

So, in other words, in order to help your child with his schooling you need to take the long view – after all, children will be in some

The stages of education

Age	Stage	Year	Statutory assessments
3–4	Early Years Foundation Stage		Early Years Foundation Stage Profile
4–5		Reception	
5–6	Key Stage 1	Year 1	
6–7		Year 2	National tests and tasks (SATs) in English and maths
7–8	Key Stage 2	Year 3	
8–9		Year 4	
9–10		Year 5	
10–11	Key Stage 3	Year 6	National tests (SATs) in English, maths and science
11–12		Year 7	
12–13		Year 8	
13–14		Year 9	National tests (SATs) in English, maths and science
14–15	Key Stage 4	Year 10	Some young people take GCSEs
15–16		Year 11	Most young people take GCSEs or other national qualifications
16–17	Sixth form (can be school or college)	Year 12 Lower Sixth/ First year college	Many young people take AS (Advanced Subsidiary) level assessments, which are stand-alone qualifications valued as half a full A level qualification.
17–18		Year 13 Upper Sixth/ Second year college	Many young people complete A level courses by taking the final year A2 assessments.

form of 'formal' education from the age of 3 (and earlier, with the latest Government curriculum laying down how children are expected to develop from birth) until they are 18 and beyond!

Good communication is key to helping you decide on an approach for the long view. Set aside time to discuss the whole issue with your partner or family – preferably a quiet space without distractions (especially children!). Don't put off this chat; you'll be amazed at how quickly your child grows up and at how the whole issue of secondary education (which is so easy to put to the back of your mind) creeps up and hits you while you're still fretting about his first football match or whether he will have a speaking part in the school nativity play.

You may well find that you and your partner occasionally disagree about your child's education and future. This is quite normal and natural as everyone has an interest in education and at times can have strong opinions about it. The important thing is to try to reach some basic principles which you both agree on and to apply these when you are thinking about your child's education.

You'll find taking the long view or the 'whole view' is especially helpful if you have children of different ages (and most parents do). When considering the question of how your child will cope at school for the first time, try to think, plan and read ahead and consider not just what your child needs now, but what the options and challenges will be at the next stage and the stage after that.

It's important to know and be forewarned about what happens later on in order to know how to act in the early days – and hopefully this is where this book can help you. Some parents get terribly upset about, say, statutory tests at age 7, but remember that children develop at different rates: some children excel early on, others show gradual improvement over a number of years. It's amazing what can happen to a child's learning when he becomes really motivated about something.

Don't forget, too, that some tests/exams are more important than others. For example, the exams at age 15 or 16 will affect your child's access to the sixth form, so you will need to carefully weigh up the actual implications of any tests or exams as they approach, but try not get anxious too far in advance.

So what is the best course of action for you to take in order to get the best for your child at school? How should you begin and how can you find an approach that you will be able to maintain?

Create the right environment

Did you know that one of the biggest influences on your child's achievement at school is you? We often believe that schools are the places where our children learn so we hand our children over and let the school get on with it. But the real key to helping your child – whatever his stage in school and whatever his level of ability – is to engage with him yourself and to get involved with his learning. Although research evidence shows that schools do, of course, have an important influence on a child's learning, the home background is recognized as a very significant indicator of future progress.

Part of this is the environment that you create for your child.

It's not what you say, it's how you say it

Creating the right environment for your child's learning means taking an active interest in what he is doing and being enthusiastic about what he tells you or shows you he is learning.

One of the important aspects of conversations that help learning is the way you talk to your child. Don't talk down to him. In some ways, too, you should treat him just as you would any other person: you show respect, you listen to what he says and you respond appropriately. The main difference is in the vocabulary you use which, of course, the child needs to be able to understand.

So what does taking an active interest mean in practical

Olly's writing

day-to-day terms? Well, it means getting excited about your child's developments – including his drawing, reading and writing and even the language he uses.

Here's an example of taking an interest in early writing:

Example 1: Early years

Early one morning Olly came and sat on the floor in our bedroom. He had a pencil and a sheet of paper and wrote the text above.

Can you work out the nursery rhyme that he was writing? (Answer at the bottom of the page). The video clip of him doing this writing showed a remarkable period of extended concentration. You can see that he had a particular readership in mind: the members of his family.

You can also see the wonderful use of invented spelling: wns (once); wiy (why); yooh (you); bcos (because). This demonstrates

1, 2, 3, 4, 5, Once I caught a fish alive.

the way that talking feeds into writing, but also how they are such different forms of language. We showed our interest by talking to him about this wonderful piece of writing, and we also kept it for him in a lever-arch file with other examples of his drawing and writing. In later years we were able to show him the video.

Example 2: Older child

You are reading the newspaper on a Sunday morning. Your twelve-year-old daughter tells you she is going to be in a pantomime.

Do you:

a) Say, 'That's nice, dear', without looking up from your newspaper?

b) Get tickets to see the show and then engage in conversation afterwards. Perhaps like this:

CHILD: Did you enjoy it?

PARENT: Very much, I really loved your second dance. And the pirate king was funny. How did you think it went?

CHILD: Well, it was pretty good, but the first dance went a bit wrong.

PARENT: Why? What happened?

I'm sure you can see the benefits of the second approach!

Parenting can be exhausting even when two people are sharing the responsibility, and it's all too easy to glaze over when your child tries to talk to you, or to let your mind wander to what's for supper or on the TV later. So try to focus when your child is talking to you – it's important that you give him 101 per cent of your attention as you listen.

Show enthusiasm for his interests, too. When your children are young, join in with their play, talk about their doodlings, drawings, written marks and the books they are looking at. How many identify with the temptation to say, 'Oh, that's really nice', and then leave it at that? Here's a different approach: just respond with simple, but good, questioning as in these examples:

Example 3: Early years

BOY: Look what I've drawn. (Points to doodle.) It's mummy.

DAD: Gosh! That's good... I like that scarf you've drawn, what colour is that?

BOY: It's red, of course!

DAD: Oh yes, mum's red scarf, I forgot. Silly me!

BOY: Silly daddy!

DAD: That's an interesting shape. Tell me about it.

BOY: It's Felix our fluffy cat.

If you have older children, talk to them about their music or the radio shows they listen to, clothes, sports, or the things they are doing at school or outside of school (even if you can't relate to some of the stuff they tell you about).

Example 4: Older child

GIRL: Dad, don't turn it down! It's Chris Moyles on Radio 1.

DAD: Oh no. Can't we listen to Terry Wogan on Radio 2? He's more soothing.

GIRL: Noooo, pleeeaase, that's so nang. Boring. Turn it back, the show's really good and that's a wicked song.

DAD: OK. Actually I like this song. What is it?

GIRL: It's the Fratellis. C'mon dad, you're so lame!

DAD: Well, maybe, but I've just found the show's webcam [*pointing at screen*] on the computer, the studio looks pretty impressive doesn't it?

GIRL: Wow. Is that where he works? It does look cool.

DAD: Doesn't it? Anyway, you guys better get a move on or you'll miss the school bus.

Being positive (as in the example above) is not as easy as it sounds. In fact, it's quite difficult in the day-to-day melee of family life with all its natural tensions. You will find there are times when you have to really kick yourself and remind yourself to be positive. (Some people suggest using a ratio of at least five positives to every negative.) Parent-child relations are just as volatile and quixotic as any other, and this might not be helped if you're one of those parents who holds grudges, as this will make it very difficult for you to shake yourself out of a downward spiral.

So always look for positive things to say, such as:

- ✪ Thank you for taking your plate into the kitchen.
- ✪ Your hair looks nice.
- ✪ I really appreciate you saying sorry.

Sometimes it can also really help if you say, 'I'm sorry I was wrong'. (One of the most difficult things to admit to!)

How do you encourage your child?

All parents have instinctive abilities to bring up their children well but some have more time and space to reflect on how to help their child than others. But no matter how good we are as a parent we can all learn more, and inevitably we will make some mistakes.

The problem for parents who think they have it sussed (as far as organizing their children at home with creative play, a homework routine, or the like), is that they can forget about all-important communication. Yes, encouraging your child does involve having toys or games he can play with or use independently, but you will also have to join in with him from time to time, talk to him about what he is doing and, hopefully, take him forward in the things that emerge from this play. For example, if your child was making something with Lego you could sit with him on the floor and chat. If he needs your help you are there. Sometimes you might build something yourself to fit with what he is doing, or show him a new technique, such as how to put wheels on a car. This could have the advantage of helping him understand more about cars, but just interacting with him like this is part of building a good relationship.

Attitudes

The attitudes you hold and your beliefs about how your child will learn are important. Some attitudes to learning are more likely to help than others. Here are some to think about.

Encouraging, not pressurizing

It is is a good idea to encourage your child to find things to do that he is particularly interested in. The key word here is 'encourage', which means not pressurizing. However, some things in life do require sustained and regular hard work. For instance, if your child shows an ability to play a musical instrument, he will need to practise regularly to achieve each grade exam, if he wishes to do so.

Obviously, if your child shows a special aptitude for something, you need to learn to draw a balance between encouraging that talent for his benefit or for yours. It can be difficult to find the balance between goal-obsessed ambitions and encouraging your child to enjoy the moment and, sadly, many parents think only about 'hot-housing' their child. Children can be pushed too far into areas their parents deem to be best for them, so don't be a pushy parent. Yes, it's healthy to have high expectations of your child, but at the same time it is also important to be a good listener and to understand where he's coming from and where he wants – or doesn't want – to go in life.

Informed opinions

Some parents have very set views about the school their children attend; often based on almost no 'on-site' information whatsoever. How can they know if they don't go in and talk to teachers or to the headteacher? It is all too easy to form networks of opinion in the playground without proper information and, of course, there is the natural inclination to back up a child regardless of what the teacher is saying. This is a natural defence mechanism that's quite 'primal'.

But it is important to form your opinions on the basis of valid evidence, not just on discussion with other parents in the playground.

Talk the talk

The way a parent talks to their child is an important part of supporting learning. For example, how much should you correct your child? Over-correcting him, particularly when the 'mistakes' are part of normal development, is not a good thing. For example, a young child who says 'I goed to the shops' is showing a perfectly normal and logical way of learning the English language. On the other hand, if your child was really struggling to read simple picture books that other children could read at age 6, you might want to think about this and take advice from the school.

A word or two on pushy parents

Most parents are in admiration of their children's teachers and the fact that they have to deal with 30-plus children, day-in and day-out, especially if the parent can admit how hard it can be to deal with just one, two or three children. However, some parents will insist that they know best and are incredibly pushy about exercising their rights when it comes to supporting or protecting their child at school. This pushiness may be more about style than substance but, as a rule of thumb, how should you approach teachers?

The best way to deal consistently with schools is to 'box clever': that is, you've got to appreciate the constraints that teachers work under, but then you've got to hold on to your concerns and be prepared to ask difficult questions (many people don't like to make a fuss). You have the right to expect informed, professional answers from the school – they won't be

Everything is mediated through talk: whatever activity you engage in with your child, indoors or outdoors, you need to offer positive praise where appropriate and to genuinely interact with your child at his level. Don't be patronizing; engage with him at his level and enjoy his company.

Encouraging ambitions

'Reach for the clouds and you'll hit the tree tops.'

This expression means that if you have high expectations you may achieve your dreams. But even if you don't completely achieve them, just striving for them will have gone a long way to taking you there. However, while your expectations can guide the way you interact with your children and impact on their success at school,

simple answers though, because, of course, learning is not a simple thing.

Ultimately, as a parent, you have to take a much more positive and pro-active role in your child's education and find out what's going on by attending his school as often as you can. Parent-teacher evenings, school plays and performances, fundraising events, sports matches, and so on, are the key scheduled points of contact between parents and staff at the school; but there is also much to be learned simply from regular contact at the daily drop-off and pick-up of younger children at the school gates.

If you do have an issue with the school that you want to raise or respond to, then you need to do it in an appropriate fashion – high levels of criticism delivered in a boorish fashion are no good to anybody.

be careful of skewering this into becoming the *Fast Show*-style 'competitive dad'!

Also, as a parent you do need to think about what's likely to be the next step that will take your child forward, and whether you are prepared to take a risk on it. And that's not easy (which is where this book should come in handy). Why not assume he will go on to study at university? This book is about education; education is a lifelong process and we're looking towards university as an important stepping stone on this route. However, don't let the assumption become something that you insist on or that leads you to set such high stakes that if he doesn't get there, he feels like a failure.

So the message is: expectation is fine, but don't crank it up too much. Enthusiasm and encouragement are far better. At the same time, recognize that there are many other routes that can be fascinating and can make them very happy and successful. Classically, there are those who don't do well at school but find a niche in life that catapaults them to great business or artistic success. Businessman John Madejski (who owns Reading Football Club and its stadium – the huge Madejski Stadium) got bored at various state and private schools and, he is reported as saying: 'When you're bored you mess about. I never passed an exam. Most people – and quite rightly – pay attention and work hard... whereas people like me are more inclined to have a go at anything. I put my success [he's worth £350 million] down to going to the university of life in my early twenties.'

The other attitude to develop is *never give up*. A story from *The Observer* illustrates what is possible:

> *Retired Oxford window-cleaner Frederick Simpson, 86, has had his first book of poetry published, after writing from the age of 18.* Threads, *the achievement of a lifetime's ambition, contains 150 poems.*
>
> (OBSERVER – SEPTEMBER 2000)

Encouraging risk-taking

Children need to develop their independence and the only way they can do this is to experience new situations which will involve some risk, be it the adventure park, a concert, going into town for the first time, and so on. Sadly, in our risk-averse society, schools worry about litigation while we become more fearful about letting our children out of our sight. Of course there are risks, but these are frequently exaggerated. For example, do you think it's more dangerous for children on our roads now than it was 30 years ago? Well, the statistics tell us that it is not: the number of child deaths has in fact reduced by 75 per cent since the 1970s.

It is very important for your child's self-confidence that you encourage him to do things independently, commensurate with his stage of development and his age. For example, when do you say that he can go into the town centre with a friend on his own? Perhaps it could be in his first year of secondary school. Or when should you encourage him to walk to school on his own or ride his bike to school? (This latter question, however, is a key issue because it also brings in other current issues about the environment.)

Of course, the answers to these questions depend on the safety of the roads to your child's school and other local factors, but children in their final year of primary would seem an ideal year group to be given increased independence – especially as many of them take school-organized cycling road safety courses.

Activities

Activities are the context in which learning can take place, as they provide the perfect environment for interaction with your child. Let's look at the kinds of activities that you can organize at home and the conversations about them that might take place.

Everyday resources

Books provide an endless source of learning, and not least because they play a vital role in supporting children learning to read, so try to provide an accessible bookshelf or other place for your child's books either in his bedroom or play area. For more advice on reading and writing, as well as reading-book recommendations, see *How to Help your Child Read and Write* (see Resources, page 190).

Checklist
1 Writing and drawing tools

You should also have resources for writing and colouring pictures at home, such as various kinds of paper, pencils, crayons, child-friendly sharpeners, pens and erasers. These reading and writing tools provide opportunities for you to engage with your child's activities and for him to learn independently.

2 Toys

Start with bright, tactile toys, such as building blocks, that encourage hand-eye coordination, a sense of balance and achievement, plus the fun of knocking down a high stack! From there it's toys such as letter-box shapes in boxes and chunky 3-D jigsaws to dolls, toy cars, dressing up costumes, beany babies, bob-it, Duplo and Lego, and so on. The world's your oyster, basically you just need anything that encourages play but that can also be used as a means to interact with your child.

3 Art

Start with early-learning crayons and chalk, then move on to poster paints, which are completely washable, and non-toxic paints. When children get older and wiser, then it's time to bring out the watercolour and oil-based sets. This painting activity speaks for itself, both as a learning tool and as a means for expression and conversation. For 11-plus children you could try exploring digital images or video clips (via mobile phones or cameras) and perhaps how to use pictures in other ways, for example by exploring stop-frame animation with a home computer.

4 Involving children in cooking

This is fun and interactive and, yes, it's messy too, so have cooks' aprons ready and plenty of kitchen wipes. You can buy some great children's cookbooks these days which show the child photographically step-by-step what to do, or with wacky artwork which explains the recipes and what they are trying to achieve. Let your child measure out the ingredients, as this is a great way to learn and talk about numbers. You need to set aside a decent amount of time for this activity, which should also be at a convenient point in the day when you are not in a rush, because it requires your time and expertise, too!

5 Music to listen to

From the first music player that plays nursery rhymes to keyboarding computer-aided music technology and everything in between, such as sharing CDs and downloads, music appreciation is a fantastic activity to stimulate learning and discussion. You can also explore music and music-download websites as well as myriad pre-teen and music magazines which will feature the best-selling and most popular artists.

6 TV programmes to share

Television can be a communal and shared experience (just look at *The Royle Family!*), so rather than dismissing it as wasteful use of time or employing it as an electronic baby-sitter, recognize that some programmes can be enjoyed together as a learning experience, depending on your child's age and development. For example, popular voting-shows, such as *X Factor,* or charity

The 'glued-to-the-screen' debate

On the subject of screens and routine, you also need to manage how long and for what continuous duration you will allow your child to watch the TV or play at the computer.

Here are three key ideas:

✪ Take an interest in the technology and content.

✪ Try and 'mediate' the content so that you and your child can separate the good from the bad.

✪ Avoid a simplistic knee-jerk reaction, such as 'it's all dangerous and must be switched off'.

Parents are naturally anxious about their children watching too much TV or being glued for too long in electronic gaming or internet chat rooms – but how much is too much? Children's use of electronic media is far from all bad. Some research has shown positive outcomes for this kind of play: it is not always a solitary activity and it can help to develop hand-eye coordination. Current government guidelines suggest an individual should use a screen for no more than 50 minutes before taking a break.

With television there is also the emotive issue as to what is 'good' TV for children: *Hollyoaks* has its advocates just as much as *Blue Peter*. Parent or child alike, we're all in danger of overuse, so the key determinate here should be a mix of passive solitary pastimes with more family-shared activities.

Whatever approach you take, you should monitor your child's use of the television and only limit it if you feel it's getting excessive, perhaps if he starts to go pale and look wan! Yes, TV and computers are a resource that needs to be managed and allowed but, ultimately, passive screen gazing, even when combined with family conversation, is no substitute for active play, indoors and out.

fundraiser telethons including *Red Nose Day*, can involve family interaction and generate conversation, and possibly even learning.

Playing

Play is an important source of fun and learning at all stages of a child's development. The important point about play, from a parent's perspective, is that you have to ensure it happens. Much of children's play is spontaneous and doesn't cost anything to organize. Frequently it will involve their own role-play scenarios with siblings and friends. From time to time you may be lucky enough to take on a character and you will certainly need to be an enthusiastic audience member! Other play will require you to purchase and organize the 'play things' needed.

Indoor play

✪ **Board games**: Sitting on the floor or around a table playing board games is a great way of using your home for family learning – especially when you have more than one child. In our modern electronic age, traditional board games have been somewhat sidelined, which is a shame, because by playing them you can start the engaging-and-encouragement process very early on.

✪ **Games for young children**: From pre-school age, toys and games share many similarities. Toys and games include jigsaws; soft toys; sticking and matching activities; 'post-box' games where the child drops in the correct shapes (square, circle, star) – don't forget to praise him each time he gets an object into its designated hole. Then you can move on to other hand-eye and motor control coordination games, such as Operation®, Buckaroo®, Pop-Up Pirate® and the like, all of which encourage your child's motor skills, his ability to take turns and his sense of having fun together.

✪ **Word-building and spelling games** These include I-Spy with my little eye, Hangman, word searches, Double Quick®, Scrabble® and Boggle®.

✪ **Strategy games** Among these are 0s and Xs, Ludo, Nine Men's Morris, Draughts, Chess and Mastermind®.

✪ **Card games** These include snap, fish, cheat, whist and many many more (see the Waddington book of card games).

✪ **Board games for older children** Among these are Monopoly®, Cluedo®, The Game of Life® and The Really Nasty Horse-Racing Game® which teach 'turn-taking' ability, i.e. how to take turns, as well as how to respond to winning and losing. These games provide an inclusive little world in which you can manage such life lessons as competition, which will become part of your child's school life and prepare him for adult life too.

If the games you play are ones you were keen on as a child, this creates a history – and this also gives your child more information about you. You can tell him how you played it with your father or grandparents, and by doing so you can open up a whole new area for conversation and involvement.

Outdoor play

Games such as football or frisbee, or just throwing and catching a tennis ball in the park, are great ways to interact outdoors, or, even simpler, try climbing games or using slides in the garden or local park. These sorts of activities will help prepare your child for school events such as sports days, and you can help him to understand and deal with issues such as winning and losing, team play, rules and boundaries. When you do get to the stage of attending school sports days, the important thing for you is to turn up, be there, support him vocally and to respond to his success or defeat with equal emotional support.

Trips outside

Activities outside the house, for example, a trip to a museum or country house (whether homework-related or topic-based or not), or a visit to the movies together, provide a fantastic opportunity to build on the experience and develop your relationship with your child. Just pause and think of all the places you could take your children, even if they are just in your local area. For instance, do you have a local:

- ✪ library?
- ✪ art gallery?
- ✪ swimming pool/leisure centre?
- ✪ farm shop with livestock?
- ✪ museum?
- ✪ animal sanctuary?
- ✪ nature conservation area?
- ✪ skateboard park?
- ✪ theatre/arts centre?

All these sites represent an opportunity for stimulation and enjoyment and support in learning about the world and the community in which your child lives.

Again, conversation is key to the success of doing these activities, and the key to unlocking more interaction, involvement and understanding with your child. Moreover, by going to places that are out of the ordinary you are breaking free from the in-home routines, and this in itself can be exciting for the child and can stimulate a thirst for learning.

The library is a brilliant place for doing just this because it not only has children's books and activity area, but also often a CD and DVD lending service. Libraries also often run events such as story-telling or reading. Browsing the shelves, preferably on a regular, say, weekly or fortnightly basis, is an excellent way to broaden your child's horizons.

All the locations above offer the opportunity for:

- ✪ informal learning
- ✪ the chance to talk

✪ extending your child's knowledge-base

And, crucially, all these activities will impact on a child's ability to absorb knowledge when he is back in the classroom at school.

Encouraging interests and hobbies

Making special trips outside of the home will also help to encourage your child to develop interests and hobbies. Your child's early experiences with a wide range of activities might lead to him developing preferences for some things more than others, but whatever it is, encouraging, taking interest in and supporting his interests is what is important. Although too much specialism too soon risks a narrow perspective on life, in general it is a good thing for children to develop some skills or interests in greater depth.

If one or other parent has a special talent, say, playing the cello or being really good at tennis, they can become a role model for their child. A child might well decide very early on that he wants to play the violin if both his parents do, so then it's up to the parents to think about how they handle this. Do they want their child to go to a specialist music school? Will this narrow his experiences too soon? These are not easy questions to answer, but asking them in the context of how best to support his interests is important.

Many parents, for example, have children who are mad keen on football, and your child may even tell you that his ambition is to be a footballer. Football these days is an incredibly competitive business with some children being spotted by scouts when they are as young as eight years old. It would be tempting to dissuade your child if he was, say, only an average player, but the thing to remember is that, although not many children achieve the dizzy heights of the premiership clubs, football as a business offers many related opportunities which, later in life, might be reached by further study in sports science, for example, or physiotherapy or marketing.

Apart from the '*reach for the clouds*' philosophy, the encouragement to follow interests in depth develops the kind of thinking that is needed if your child is to do well in the education system.

Maintaining boundaries

To create the right environment at home, which will support your child at school, it helps if these two ingredients are right:

1 Behaviour
2 Routines

Routines and 'rules' – a framework for acceptable behaviour

Within the framework of creating a positive environment for your child, you have to construct clear rules as to what you, as parents, consider acceptable behaviour. Whatever age he is, you need to present your child with clear boundaries which are consistently applied. It's important to stress that this isn't simply about saying 'no' and 'don't'; there is also a positive message to get across: that you love your child and want to reward him for all the good responses but, at the same time, parental control is a 'whole package' that has to balance 'rewards' for sticking to the rules with sanctions for breaking them.

For the best chance of success with behaviour, it's a good idea to keep it simple and have just a small number of rules which can easily be remembered – say not more than five. Try to involve your child in deciding what these rules should be. You may find that you want to write down formally the rules, rewards and sanctions, as this formality shows that you mean business, but most of the time it should not be necessary to have things written down.

These rules should be expressed as positive statements, for example:

If you are going through a period when you are struggling with your child's behaviour, then good ways to check his behaviour on a daily basis is to reward him each time he shows good behaviour by giving him marbles to put in a jar or getting him to colour in a square on a chart. Five squares or marbles might be a good day, none shows a bad day.

We are polite to each other.

This means that we do not answer back; we do not say rude things; we do not make fun of each other; we do not argue unnecessarily; we say sorry without being asked and we say 'please' and 'thank you'.

We are helpful.

We set and clear the table; we do not leave things that we have used for other people to tidy up for us; we do what we are asked when we are asked and without a fuss.

Rewards to encourage good behaviour

Rewards are an excellent way to accentuate the positive and they can mirror at home what schools do in a more informal way. Both primary and secondary schools have reward systems which the parent may have no knowledge of until their child comes back with a 'well done' star or even a money voucher. In fact, secondary schools can have quite intricate systems, with various stages of awards given out and topped with a voucher, book token or cash.

So if your child comes back with a 'well done' sticker, what should you do? Straight off you need to say, '*Wow, this is fantastic*'. Explicit, positive verbal feedback is crucial in creating that nurturing home environment.

On the home front, providing some kind of treat from time to time, as well as the day-to-day praise you give, is an important part of being positive. This should still be tied in with your child adhering to the rules, but it allows a way of fashioning his behaviour in positive ways – and rewards are a very important part of that.

Here's a list of consequences of good behaviour which includes rewards. Notice that the first reward is an intrinsic one – children are happier if they stick to the rules, and so is the family.

✪ We all feel happier.

✪ We get praise:
You did a brilliant job there!
Thank you for clearing your things away.
I'm so pleased with the way you worked for that exam.
That was lovely the way you looked after your brother.

✪ Pocket money
Pocket money is not an automatic right: it should perhaps be seen more as fair payment and reward for good behaviour and at times for a child's hard work helping around the home. If chores are not done, or if behaviour is not acceptable, withholding pocket money can be very persuasive! However, beware of the temptation to use money simply as a bribe.

✪ Choice of meal
As parents we tend to plan the meals for our children so that they are as healthy as possible and provide all the nutritional requirements they need to grow. So, as children often don't get much choice over what they are going to eat, allowing them a choice every now and again can be quite a good reward.

✪ Treat
This could be as simple as having a luxurious ice cream, or it might be to stay up a bit later one night, or perhaps a magazine or small toy or some extra pocket money.

○ Special event

Ask your children where they would like to go: it might be ten-pin bowling, or it might be a theme park visit. Although these trips can be good for all sorts of things, there's no harm in saying to your

Rewards and consequences consistently applied

Whether applying rules, rewards or consequences, the key is to do it consistently. The methods of encouraging good behaviour discussed here are ones often used by schools and teachers too, which means that your child will understand his school's expectations because he will have learned them at home, which in turn will help him to learn better.

One effective way of encouraging older children is to engage them in the drafting of the 'rules'. In other words, ask them what they are looking for and what might work for them, rather than unilaterally laying down the law which might only provoke resistance and arguments.

When setting up routines, watch out for any slippage: a child may try to subvert the rules and sometimes you'll forget to enforce them; but do remember that the management of rules and routines is not something you will solve in one go and then leave.

At the end of the day this approach is all about trying to achieve the behaviour you want from your child and the strategies you use to get it, and in that scenario, of course, building a good relationship is fundamental. (To find out more in what is a vast topic of practical parenting, check out *Little Angels* and *Teen Angels* – see Resources, page 190.)

child, '*I want to take you somewhere special because you have been good for such a long time*'.

Sanctions for bad behaviour

While accentuating the positive side to parenting you also need to spell out to your child how parenting also involves drawing up sanctions for bad behaviour. These can include:

1 A warning.

2 A telling off.

3 Being sent to his bedroom.

4 Denying a minor privilege, e.g. no computer, TV, electronic games for a day.

5 Denying a major privilege, e.g. not seeing friends or an activity cancelled.

Routines

✪ **Bedtime** Some kind of bedtime routine is vital, especially in the younger years. It is absolutely essential that children and teenagers get enough sleep – you see many children going to school looking tired and slothful and insufficient sleep will not help their ability to learn, let alone get through the day!

✪ **Breakfast time** Create a morning routine with sufficient time for a good breakfast, even if the whole family doesn't necessarily sit round the table. First thing in the morning is inevitably a rushed part of the day but it needn't be stressful; sustenance at that time is critical for a child's performance in class – particularly when they reach 11 o'clock and still have an hour or so before the next meal. Research has shown that children nosedive before 11 o'clock if they haven't eaten a reasonable breakfast – at least a drink of fruit juice, cereal and milk, or toast, but it could be porridge or even the occasional treat of bacon and egg!

At secondary school level, stopping off at the newsagent's to buy fizzy drinks, crisps or a chocolate bar is not going to give a child sufficient energy to keep concentration levels going till the next 'fuelling stop' of lunch. Schools recognize this, which is why more and more are taking up 'breakfast clubs', especially in areas where children are not encouraged to have a decent breakfast at home.

For the breakfast routine at home a 'no screens' policy (no TV, DVD or computer games) can be good. This allows more opportunity for family interaction to discuss the day ahead and plans for later, and can be a highly successful strategy for parents.

✪ **Tea and evening mealtimes**. It's really important that parents organize these parts of the day to ensure they regularly have some meals with their children. After all, it's quite rare these days that the family comes together and has a chance to talk. That could be tea and toast watching *Neighbours*, together with a quick, 'How was school?' or, 'What did you learn today?', before the children disperse to do homework or chill out in their rooms, or it could be a half-hour supper around the kitchen table where the children have set the table and then help with the clearing or washing up. Tie this in with rewards (see pages 36–9).

> **Managing mealtimes can be a very successful strategy for keeping a space in the day to talk about school or just stuff with your child. It may not be possible to do this every weekday evening, but creating the sense of settling into a routine before or after school is fundamental to giving him a sense of continuity through term time and can be continued in the holidays.**

Punctuality

Which home sounds familiar?

Scenario 1

9pm (the night before school) The parents flop in front of TV. The children's homework is not finished and next day's school clothes are still on a pile by the washing machine.

6.45am The alarm doesn't goes off (the child's or the parents').

7.15 Child wakes up; everyone is 15 minutes late so there's a rush for the bathroom.

7.30 Dad wanders about to make tea but actually doesn't help in any way.

Cries of '*Where is my uniform?*', '*Where is my sports bag?*'

7.45 Mum tries to finish off yesterday's homework. Toast burns. Smoke alarm goes off. The breakfast table looks like a war zone: all the cupboards are open and worksurfaces are littered with breakfast debris. Children brush their teeth wherever they can.

7.50 Children rush to catch the school bus leaving packed lunch and bags behind.

Scenario 2

7pm (the night before school) Homework finished, reading book read and comments book filled in.

8pm Next day's clothes are laid out – washed and ironed. Lunch-box sandwich ready in fridge. Breakfast table is laid.

6.45am Parents' alarm goes off and one or both parents are up and ready and waiting by 7am.

7.00 Wake up children.

7.15–7.30 Everyone down and having breakfast.

7.50 Children leave to catch bus, hair combed, teeth brushed, and dirty dishes have been put in the sink.

Your scenario is probably a bit of both of these two; while some parents go for the military operation approach, something a little less joyless is preferable. But whichever routine works for you, there should always be room for negotiation – and routine is something that has to be worked at.

Obviously, the key thing here is that getting a child to school on time is an absolute must; lots of children arrive at school late on a regular basis, and that's not doing them any favours and will get the parents into trouble too!

Homework

The requirements of a school will probably first directly impact on the home when your child appears with homework. Homework is so important to your child's education that the government lays down targets about it, for example, from ages 5 to 7, children should have at least 1 hour a week, covering reading, spelling and number work, and this increases through the years (see Chapter 2 for a more detailed breakdown).

At the age of 5 years old your child will just be bringing home a reading book, probably in a wallet with a note book or reading diary. The expectation (from the school) is that the parent will read with the child, telling the story and saying and pointing at the words and pictures. Often the parent will be expected to write a note in the reading diary about how this went. Once this starts, a routine then needs to be established by the parent to do this every day, preferably at the same point in the day (before bed is usually the best time) or at least to have a fairly regular slot.

It cannot be stressed enough that homework is one of the most important things you can do with your child, and your role here is to set the boundaries as to when it should be done. For example:

✪ Do you want them to do homework straight away, effectively to continue the school day a little while longer?

✪ Will it be before other activities, such as going on the internet?

✪ Would you prefer to give them a break from school before they start homework?

Whichever slot you go for, when it comes to homework, make sure it is a regular one.

You might also need to work out how homework will fit in around your child's other after-school activities, such as sport, music and things like Brownies and Cubs (it should not replace other after-school activities, though). But don't worry, this is a subject we will address in the next few chapters; suggesting ways in which you can help your child, as well as the dos and don'ts of doing so.

parents and school

New school, new choices

Whether you have just moved to a new area, or you are already there, you need to know what the local provisions for learning are like. How do you know how good the local provision is during the early years, primary, secondary, or sixth form level? You will probably want to know which schools provide the best academic results. Your child might have particular needs that some settings will provide for better than others, so you will need to know which ones are best; or she might have particular talents, such as in music. These are all important matters which will have an impact on your child's development, so in order to make an informed choice you need to have the best information to hand.

So where do you start looking?

Gathering information

The internet offers a rich source of information about education, but you need to know which are the best websites. In this chapter (and throughout the book) we recommend the most reliable and authoritative sites which will help you find out more about your child's education. All the relevant addresses are listed in the Resources section on page 183.

'Directgov', for example, is a public service website which has a section devoted to education and learning. It lists the options for primary and secondary schools in your area, as well as for local 'care', including childminders, nurseries, crèches, playgroups, children's day-care providers, nursery education, out-of-school clubs and holiday play schemes. You can find information on individual schools' achievements and attainment, maps and contact details for all these pre-school and out-of-school childcare options.

The official Ofsted site (see Resources for website address) also provides excellent information for parents on precisely how to

What is Ofsted?

The new Ofsted – the Office for Standards in Education, Children's Services and Skills – came into being on 1 April 2007. This non-ministerial government department (which means it doesn't report to government ministers but directly to Parliament, and to the Lord Chancellor about children and family courts administration) brings together the wide experience of four formerly separate inspectorates that inspect and regulate care for children and young people, as well as inspecting education and training for learners of all ages.

Ofsted carries out hundreds of inspections and regulatory visits each week. Ofsted's school reports, in particular, primarily focus on education provision, but they also try to give a 'snapshot' of the whole establishment in terms of teaching and caring and take into account the backgrounds of the children who attend the school. Because Ofsted does not report to government ministers, it does claim to have some independence. However, Ofsted also works closely with partners and stakeholders – including government departments and other agencies – to make sure that its inspection and regulation is used to realize their vision.

find suitable education provision, based on their reports, within a five- to 20-mile radius of your postcode (key that bit in when requested). From 'care' to education, the site is a superb useful starting point.

The main reason for starting your search for information on the Ofsted site is that you will find detailed reports about schools and other educational settings there, and there are also links to statutory test results. After all, it makes much more sense to check a school report BEFORE you visit that school, because then you will be visiting it with some idea in your head of what to expect and, crucially, what to ask head teachers and teachers about.

Using Ofsted reports online

In order to find the inspection report for a school that you would like your child to attend you need to go to the Ofsted website. From there you can use your postcode to search for schools within the distance that you set.

Once you click on the name of the school you are interested in, you will be presented with a page which lists some basic information such as a section from a local map showing the location of the school, contact details, and so on. The hyperlinks to inspection reports (including the most recent and, if appropriate, previous reports) allow you to read the current Ofsted report for the school. There is also a hyperlink to statistics in relation to how the school performed in the statutory tests.

Ofsted reports consist of various sections:

✪ Basic information on the first page.

✪ Description of the school, including socio-economic information, such as the number of children receiving free school meals and children with English as an Additional Language (EAL).

✪ The key for inspection grades: 1=outstanding; 2=good; 3=satisfactory; 4=inadequate.

✪ Overall effectiveness of the school.

✪ Achievement and standards.

✪ Personal development and wellbeing.

✪ Quality of provision regarding teaching and learning; curriculum and other activities; care, guidance and support; leadership and management.

✪ Appendices, including a more detailed breakdown of grades for different sections and the letter to pupils informing them about the outcome of the inspection.

The inspection system, like the whole education system, is strongly influenced by the outcomes of statutory tests (see page 52). This is why, following the summary section 'overall effectiveness', the section 'achievement and standards' comes first in any inspection report.

If a school is achieving test scores that are at the national average or above then it is very unlikely that it would fail an inspection. However, schools that are not achieving national standards, and whose standards are significantly below similar schools, are likely to come under intense scrutiny as part of the inspection. If a school fails an inspection it will be put under 'special measures', something that triggers extra support from the local authority (LA) and more frequent monitoring inspections.

Sample Ofsted report 1: School in York, 2007

The school is judged by the reporting inspector to be outstanding. This is made clear from the opening sentences in the section about overall effectiveness:

> *'This is an outstanding school where every child is nurtured and valued, summarized in the display in the entrance where photographs of pupils are linked to where their families are from on a map of the world. ... Progress is excellent because of the high quality of teaching and pupils reach average standards by the time they leave in Year 6.'*

Although the school was only graded 3 (i.e. satisfactory) in the category 'The standards reached by learners', the inspector clearly felt that the school was achieving high standards, in view of the low attainment from which the children started school. This was indicated by the following quote from the report:

> *'From a very low starting point children make rapid progress in the nursery ... Pupils with English as an*

additional language have extra support with English and progress for these pupils – who often arrive at school without any English – is quite exceptional.'

Progress of this kind is known as 'value-added', because some schools achieve more than others with children who start with low attainment. The statutory test statistics now include these value-added measures.

Sample Ofsted report 2: School in Worcester, 2007

This school had been in 'special measures', which meant that it was required to have further monitoring inspections. Its report is based on one of these monitoring inspections. Here's what the inspector wrote about achievement and standards:

'Standards remain exceptionally low. Although the 2006 national assessments show Year 2 pupils did better in reading than the previous year, none of them reached the higher Level 3 and overall attainment fell. However, Year 6 national test results indicate that standards are rising slowly. That said, standards of writing across the school are still an area of great concern. Lesson observations and a scrutiny of pupils' work, as well as the school's own data, indicate the majority of pupils are making inadequate progress in their writing skills.'

The best features of Ofsted reports are when they simply describe what they have seen on the basis of the evidence they have collected. Problems can arise when this turns to making sweeping judgments about what the school should do to improve. For example, in this same report it is said that:

'Good progress is made in lessons when teaching is enthusiastic and inspiring.'

Well, few people would argue with that insight! But the problem
is that the inspection system has been, in part, responsible for
encouraging less than inspiring teaching over the years.

In the same paragraph of the report there is a clue as to why
this is:

> *'Teachers' lesson plans for English, mathematics
> and science are detailed. They contain clear learning
> objectives, tasks at different levels of difficulty, and
> ways of assessing pupils' achievements. Nevertheless,
> the content is sometimes based on what national
> guidelines suggest is appropriate for pupils of certain
> ages, rather than what is needed for individuals and
> groups of pupils in the class. This means that pupils
> lose interest, move off task and make little progress.
> Examples of this were seen at the start of literacy
> lessons where pupils sat for too long while the purpose
> of the lesson was introduced and explained.'*

Since 1997 there has been very strong pressure from the
government through the inspection system to base teaching on
'national guidelines' such as the national literacy strategy. These
guidelines clearly specify in very particular terms what teachers
must teach in every year of primary school, but this has frequently
resulted in a narrow and uninspiring curriculum.

It is ironic, to say the least, that in the light of years of
pressure in the opposite direction, this inspection report should
suggest that teaching should now be based more on pupil's needs
and interests and less on national guidelines.

This problem is also caused, in part, by not rigorously
separating cause from effect. There are many variables which
contribute to why a school is not achieving high standards; some
of these are:

1 Pupils' experiences prior to coming to school.

Tests and tables – what do they all mean?

You will probably have come across the term SATs; these are the statutory tests taken by children in school (see table on page 16 to see when they are taken). SAT is actually a copyright term, owned by an American organization, which originally stood for Scholastic Achievement Test. For this reason, in this book, we use the more accurate phrase 'statutory tests'.

Parents are aware of how the 'target-setting agenda' has become the norm for both workplace and school. English schools test their children more than any other country in the world. The statutory tests that your child will carry out throughout their schooling are used to compare the effectiveness of schools (the nature of the tests and tasks is explained more fully in Chapters 4 and 5.) This has resulted in league tables appearing in national media.

The league tables, posted via newspapers or websites,

2 The socio-economic background of the pupils.
3 Individual pupils' capabilities and motivation at different times in their schooling.
4 The quality of the head teacher and the management system.
5 The quality of the teachers and the teaching.
6 The links with the local community.
7 The teaching methods used.

Researchers know how difficult it is to attribute particular factors to pupils' attainment outcomes. When looking at inspection reports for schools in your area the most useful information is the descriptive details contained in the reports and, in particular, the comments about the overall effectiveness of the school. As mentioned earlier, are designed around such eye-catching headings as 'Best and worst GCSE results', 'Schools who are best or worst at "adding value"', 'Most-improved schools', 'Top A level results', and so on. It's not unlike the football league tables. Some schools emphasize preparation for tests much more than others. As a parent, you can ask them how much time is spent on this.

So, are these tests actually there to help the children? Well, no, not really, they're as much about accountability and monitoring schools as about assessing children's learning. There is a growing feeling that the disadvantages of the testing system outweigh the advantages.

So, when considering a school, you should not make your decision about it solely on the outcome of tests. If you realize that tests are not the only measure of a child's progress – or a school's success – then this will prompt you to take account of a wider range of information.

you should read such information but then combine it with your impressions from a visit to the school. So while Ofsted information is useful, it needs to be considered in conjunction with other sources, including the impressions you have formed yourself after you have visited the school.

Weighing it all up

Bear in mind that when researching the options for local education you are trying to get an overview of them; an early years setting, a school, or a sixth form is not just about league tables and test results. It is also important that you find out about other things, such as the school ethos, facilities for extra-curriculum activities, the school environment and children's demeanour at school, the relationship of that school with others it feeds into – and these elements can only be confirmed by actually visiting the provider of your choice.

Remember, statutory test scores are just one measure of the 'progress' of a school: it's quite possible that a school which has scores close to or a little below the national average happens to have a very good Ofsted report because the children are coming in at a lower level or at base line because of their socio-economic background. In other words, the school is doing very well to move them forward but is still going to find it hard to get above the national averages. It's also possible that you find a school with very high test results that still doesn't work for your child. This may be because your child isn't inspired by the teachers, because the school is 'coasting' or because the children are predominantly from a better-off socio-economic background and are extremely well supported at home (which means that this school is therefore not adding as much value as it would for families unable to provide this support).

When choosing your educational provider, other key issues for consideration are access to it and convenience for transport – for example, is it within walking distance? There are also myriad personal factors which will have an impact on your decision, factors that only you can answer.

Schools are required to update a 'school profile' by the end of July each year. This profile offers a range of useful information for parents, which includes the school's successes, what the school is trying to improve, pupil progress, change in results over time, and a range of broader factors indicating the quality of the school. There should be a link to the profile from any school website but you may also find a link by going to the DirectGov website and then to the 'find school' or 'schools finder' section. (See Resources on page 183 for the website address.)

School and local authority websites

If one education setting in particular takes your fancy you can visit its website (most have them) which will give you further insight and visual guidance about the establishment.

Local authority websites will also have links to the care and education providers in their catchment areas. Oxfordshire, for example, provides 12 nursery schools, 234 primary schools, 34 secondary schools, 14 special schools and 500 early years and childcare settings. Its website lists useful information for parents about schools in Oxfordshire and the work the county council is doing to improve school performance, including term dates and contact details of all schools in the county.

Other areas of local authority sites give information on early years education, financial support, information on out-of-hours school-related activities, libraries, special education needs, student support and even advice for parents wishing to educate their children at home.

Talk about it to others

Friends, family and neighbours with nursery-age or school-age children are worth talking to to sound out any extra information on your local education provision – but be wary that they might have all sorts of issues and prejudices that may not be relevant to your needs, as well as limitations to their knowledge.

A lot of feedback is bound to be anecdotal, too. However, ask yourself this: are the people you talk to broadly happy with the school in question? Or are there quite a few who are less than happy? If this is the case, treat this as a warning signal. Again, be sensible: if feedback from local friends or neighbours is more about the school generally (veering on gossip), than about their specific child and their own direct experience, then treat the information only as reliably as it is presented.

Where the 'local network' will be particularly valuable is on practical tips such as dropping off and picking up the children, diary dates for fundraisers, seasonal fairs, coffee mornings, volunteer help. Chatting at the 'school gates' is, of course, a surefire way to meet other mums and dads and provides an opportunity to invite other children to play or have your child invited over. Talking to local parents can also be helpful as an informal network of information about whether there is bullying or a particularly unruly group of children at certain stages of the school.

Local library and council offices

The library is an excellent resource for finding schools, as well as being a learning resource. Your local council offices will also have leaflets and information about education providers in your area and can answer your initial queries about the number of schools and where they are.

School visit

Whatever factors you are trying to juggle to make your choice, there is no substitute for going to visit the places you have whittled down to fit your shortlist. Make an appointment to visit the school and, ideally, to meet the head teacher because he or she has a strong influence on its quality. The phone number of the school will be listed on its website, in the phone directory, at the library or with the local council.

What are you trying to find out?

You should use a visit to a school to see if you can be persuaded and convinced that it is the right place for your child. You can pick up so many signals from a visit: listen to the head teacher's views about education (and those of any other people that you meet) and the way they 'sell' the school.

Heads count

It is the head teacher who not only directs but also symbolizes the school's ethos: its values, its outgoing demeanour, its commitment to children, the community, extra curriculum activities, links with the local business and other educational establishments, its attitude to parent-teacher events, governors, healthy eating and myriad other issues inside and outside the school gates.

You need to be looking for a stable school with a head who's been there some time and who is keen to continually encourage improvements. Certainly if the school you are considering, or have chosen, has an acting head, it is worth asking why this is and when it is expected that the new head will take over.

A new head can often mean upheaval of a positive kind. Ideally, a new head should be selected before the old head leaves, and if the acting head has been there a long time that could be a warning signal of difficulties in making an appointment at what might be a struggling school. In general, you need to keep one eye open on issues related to staff turnover – it should neither be too speedy nor too moribund.

Here are a few pointers:

✪ Does what the head teacher tells you fit in with your outlook on learning?

✪ Is he happy to show you round the school or setting, rather than just talk in an office?

✪ Are the pupils present during your visit? It is better if they are because you can't get a proper idea of how a school works without seeing its teachers and pupils in action.

✪ Is there an opportunity to see the school and children actively engaged in class or playtime?

✪ One question you should ask at your first school meeting is how the school organizes its parents' or open evenings and what you, as a parent, should anticipate. This could be a lot more helpful than simply knowing the dates and times.

All these insights should give you a good gut reaction, although in fairness to schools they do get a lot of visitors: education publishers' reps, school dinner/canteen suppliers, prospective teachers, carers and so on – not to mention inspectors!

Here are a couple of examples of how a visit might go:

A good visit

✪ First contact: get through to relevant staff; treated to a positive and friendly phone manner in answer to your initial questions about making an appointment, and in response to any other questions.

✪ On arrival for school visit: well-signposted directions to the car park, school and entrance.

✪ Security at the school gates/reception/secretary's office. Are they prepared for your appointment?

✪ The children you see in the classrooms, playground, canteen and assembly hall generally appear happy and engaged; the environment appears settled and attractive.

✪ Condition of buildings and infrastructure appears fresh and clean and inside it is warm.

✪ There are plenty of children's drawings, posters and work, as well as school trips, commendations and well done notes visible on the walls, alongside parent-teacher info and suchlike.

✪ Reception areas and meeting rooms are welcoming.

✪ You have confidence in what the head teacher tells you about the school and you establish some rapport with him.

✪ If you are attending a more formal open evening, the welcome speech can be an important indicator: you like what you hear and the way it is presented.

A poor visit (extreme scenario!)

✪ First contact: you don't get through to a person, just an answer machine and nobody returns your call.

✪ When they do pick up, the phone manner is brusque and busy and it feels as if there are quite a few hurdles just to make an appointment.

✪ On arrival for the school visit it is not obvious where to go and the secretary doesn't seem to have details for your appointment; there is no signing-in book and you sit in a drab entrance way or lobby to wait for someone to come and get you.

✪ There is a dearth of pupils' work or drawing displayed and seems to be no reference anywhere to events, fund-raising, children's clubs, and so on.

✪ The children you see in the classrooms, playground, canteen and assembly hall appear unnaturally muted and you see a lot of children behaving very badly.

✪ Condition of buildings and infrastructure appears frayed at the edges.

✪ Reception areas and meeting rooms are unwelcoming.

✪ You disagree quite strongly with some of the head teacher's ideas, and he seems disinterested when you voice your concerns.

Ask your child

Last, but not least, having gathered as much data as possible, what does your child think about the school you like? Have you discussed with her where she might be going? Do you have a choice of schools? If so, does your daughter have a preference? Why is this?

How you involve your child in making such decisions about her life becomes more and more important as she gets older and has reasoned and considered opinions. She might prefer the smaller of two schools because it better suits her character (the other option might be quite a large school), or perhaps one of her friends is going there too (which is often an important factor). Discussing which school she likes and why is part of the learning process and you want her to become an independent thinker about her own education and what does or doesn't work for her.

Choosing a school – is it a lottery?

The local authority in the seaside resort of Brighton opted for a lottery system of allocation of places to its more popular schools. This was much to the dismay of middle-class parents who may have bought properties simply to be in the catchment area of an allegedly better-achieving school (on the premise that those living next to sought-after schools win out when more children apply to a school than has room for them).

Now the council are intending to randomly allocate places to children when a school cannot accommodate all the children who apply. This might be the beginning of a trend; new admissions codes for schools in England and Wales came into effect in 2007 to help decisions when there are competing claims. Faith, proximity and siblings still count, but very popular schools are being encouraged along the lottery route which includes a representative mix of abilities for the area, alongside entrance exams.

Parents' appeals against non-admission have risen dramatically in recent years. Ultimately, the goal of education should be about creating better schools for all, not getting bogged down in complicated admissions systems and appeals.

The private school option

A lot of the factors that mark out one state school from another apply to private schools, too. In other words, there are some very good ones and there are also some not-so-good ones.

The key factor in private education is that you pay (a lot) for your child's education in return for more generous resourcing and smaller class sizes. But smaller classes doesn't necessarily mean a better education. Again, as with state schools, the big question is how well will your child fit into and adapt to this environment? Certainly it is argued that private provision tends to have a good track record as far as getting children into universities is concerned, but schools are not all the same and they can vary tremendously in character. Ultimately, selecting the right private school will come down to individual choice and financial means.

The website of the Independent Schools Council gives further information (see Resources for website address). As far as inspection of these private schools is concerned, they are inspected by the independent schools inspectorate (ISI), as approved by the Education Act 2002. Ofsted will only inspect schools where the head teacher is **not** a member of an association that is affiliated to the Independent Schools Council. In these cases Ofsted inspects independent schools at the request of the DCSF (Department for Children, Schools and Familes) in order to ensure that they comply with The Education (Independent School Standards) Regulations 2003, which specify the provision a school should make. In inspecting these schools, Ofsted uses the powers granted by Section 162A of the Education Act 2005. For this reason independent school inspections are sometimes known as 'section 162A inspections'.

How to make the most of the links between home and school

There are several ways in which you can get more actively involved with your child's school than simply dropping her off, picking her up or asking how her day was, important though these are.

This is where you decide whether you want to take proactive steps to help your child's school in some extra capacity than just being an interested parent, such as engaging as a volunteer, parent-teacher committee member or even as a governor (see page 64). There is, of course, one particularly basic link between home and school that you can't get away from. It can creep up on you without you realizing; it can even sit inside your child's school bag for days without you knowing about it, but when you get a note, or even a call, from school asking what's happened to the book she was meant to read or the project she was meant to complete at home, then you'll know sure enough. Yes, we are talking about homework.

Homework

When your child brings homework back, this is often the first time that having a child at school really hits home, and there is much you can do as a parent to help your child. This is covered in more detail in Chapter 4, but here are a few things that can help:

✪ Ask your child if she has homework to do (which might be as straightforward as reading a book); don't expect her necessarily to volunteer this information.

✪ Ask her if there is anything you can do to help without, importantly, actually doing everything for her.

✪ Ensure you have an internet-ready, working home computer with a good supply of paper and printing ink.

✪ Ensure you have enough stationery (pens, pencils, erasers, rulers, paper glue, whitener, hole puncher, stapler and so on) and the basic references, such as dictionaries, at home.

✪ Create a comfortable, quiet place with no distractions for her to do her homework.

✪ Create an after-school routine so that homework has its natural place, ideally not too late in the day.

✪ Help your child to know which websites are reliable and help her to understand and use the information they provide.

✪ Get books from the local, or mobile, library, if time permits.

✪ Visit a local site that is relevant to the topics being studied at school, such as a Roman fort or museum with an Egyptian mummy.

Homework is critical to your child's education and an important bridge between your child, her school and your home. However, it should never replace other after-school activities such as sport and music or organized activities such as Brownies, Scouts or youth club. Homework should NOT become a stressful activity, and you should offer your child constant reassurance as she grapples with it, and praise her when she gets it right.

There are government guidelines about homework which cover the amount each year group should receive, for example:

✪ Years 1 and 2: 1 hour a week for reading, spelling, other literacy work and number work.

✪ Years 3 and 4: 1½ hours per week for numeracy and literacy and other subjects.

✪ Years 5 and 6: 30 minutes per day with a regular timetable; literacy, numeracy and other subjects too.

The guidelines for secondary school children are:

✪ Years 7 and 8: 45 to 90 minutes per day.

✪ Year 9: 1 to 2 hours per day.

✪ Years 10 and 11: 1½ to 2½ hours per day.

Getting more involved
Volunteering

Many schools welcome volunteers, but you have to be prepared to fill in a CRB check (Criminal Records Bureau) and possibly other forms even for the simplest involvement. Helping out can mean getting involved with a range of activities, from assisting on class outings, sorting out library books, helping with the scenery or costumes for the school play or being there to help at school sports days and fêtes.

Ask the school's head teacher or secretary what his policy is on parental involvement when you make your first visit. It's important to add that you should only commit to helping out if you know you have the time and temperament to do it; schools find it hard enough to manage without having volunteers reneging on their commitment.

Parent-Teacher Associations

One of the main contact points between parent and school is via the Parent-Teacher Association (PTA). This body organizes events at which both parents and children can enjoy themselves and is a very good community support-group of like-minded parents who will get together informally to raise much-needed funds for, say, more computers, a school mini-bus or for playground equipment.

Some schools also have associations which are more formally organized, with a newsletter and/or website, and which are usually affiliated to a national umbrella organization: the Confederation of Parent-Teacher Associations. These associations will usually have a committee made up of officers (a secretary, treasurer and chairperson) and ordinary members; a member of school staff may be represented, too.

If you have a child at the school you will automatically become a member of the Parent-Teacher Association, and you can put yourself forward to join the committee. The committee decides what to do and when to do it. Many events will be fundraisers (for example, tabletop fêtes, quiz nights and car boot sales); others may be social, for example, film clubs and dances.

Governors

All schools have governors. The number of these governors depends on the size of the school, but most governing bodies will include elected parents of children at the school, elected teachers, some more governors selected from the local community and some appointed from the local authority (who may or may not be governors). If your child is at a church school, the governing body will also include some representatives of the church foundation.

The role of a governor is a much more formal liaison between home and school and at their committee meetings governors will discuss and act upon issues including:

❂ Staffing the school: numbers of staff, appointments and promotions.

❂ Allocation of local authority funds.

❂ Deciding on the ethos of the school and finding ways to promote it.

❂ Monitoring and agreeing school development plans.

❂ Drawing up an action plan that must be implemented after an Ofsted inspection.

There are three main ways to become a governor. You can be:

1 Elected as a parent-governor. The school will let you know when the elections are due; all parents over the age of 18 can stand for election and they all have a vote.

2 Appointed by the local authority. Many ordinary members of the public are appointed because there are not enough councillors to go round all the schools. Contact your local authority to see if they keep a list of people who wish to be school governors and ask if you can be added to it.

3 Co-opted (selected) by the governing body as, say, a local businessperson. To qualify for this method of appointment you need to write to the governors explaining your interest and then, when there is a vacancy, they may contact you. If you are interested in a church school, contact the officials of your local church to see if this is a possibility.

If you want to get involved with your child's school, then think about the possibility of becoming a member of her school PTA or perhaps the board of governors. If the informal and social suits you then the PTA is best, but if you can handle the formal meetings and genuinely have the best interests of the whole school in mind – not just those of your child – then being a governor might be the role for you.

Parents' evenings

Whether you are on the PTA or board of governors, or neither, you should attend the parents' evenings that are laid on by schools at least once per year, and often more frequently than that.

These 'evenings' are usually held from the late afternoon until mid evening and you will be informed about when these will be in advance, most likely by a letter given to your child by her school.

How you receive this information and how it is presented will tell you much about the organization of the school. Assuming you have been given plenty of warning, do make sure that at least one parent can attend (especially if you are both working).

What should you expect?

Parents' evenings will differ in their form and function depending on the type of school and year group of your child, but in principle you should expect the following:

1 At primary school, examples of your child's work will be available for you to look through. Don't forget to pay attention to wall displays and other displays, too, because these will speak volumes about the kind of work that the school values.

2 Your child's teacher should offer some *positive* comments about her and how her learning is progressing; this is a signal that the teacher is acting professionally. His conversation with you should not start with negatives – you should always expect to hear some positive statements about your child first.

3 You should get sufficient feedback about how your child could improve her work/learning. You should be seeking evidence that he has assessed your child properly in a relatively in-depth way, and that he can tell you some quite practical ways to help her.

4 You need to listen, take in the advice and think about how you can use it to help your child.

5 You want the class teacher to talk about your child in a way that makes you feel he really knows her. Certainly at secondary level that's much more difficult for subject teachers than for primary and nursery teachers, but there is no excuse for any of them to only trot out bland, national curriculum, governmental-sounding statements that have been churned off a computer package. However, do bear in mind that schools and teachers are also under considerable government pressure to report things like national curriculum levels and statements.

6 A chance to ask your own questions – a really good teacher will ask for your opinion of your child's learning. Time is usually very tight at these events, so arrive prepared with questions that have been on your mind already. Hopefully the teachers will answer them head on and not be on the defensive. Of course, both sides need to be reasoned. Some parents find these evenings quite daunting; especially if they don't know any other parents there or are meeting the teachers for the first time.

7 If your child is at primary level you should discuss any feedback with your child after the parents' evening. If she is at secondary level, then she is likely to be present during the meetings anyway.

Checklist of questions to ask at a parents' evening

1 What's my child's strongest subject?
2 What does my child like doing?
3 What is my child good at?
4 How do her test scores/assessment results compare to national/school's/class averages?
5 How is my child doing in relation to her peers?
6 What things does my child need to work on?
7 What is my child less good at?
8 How well is my child socializing in class?
9 How well is my child socializing in playtime/freetime/meal times?

The kind of questions you ask can help you to find out a lot more about how your child is coping with learning. What you need to avoid is a parents' evening where basically you just sit there, don't say a word (and are not asked to either), while the teacher only talks to you about targets he is going to set for the rest of year.

ParentMail

In today's technological world, information is increasingly coming from schools through email and text message, via a central national site where you can register your email address.

One such site is ParentMail which, it is claimed, is used by 1,000 UK schools to communicate with parents, governors and staff by email and text message. It is a site that you need to register with, and log on with a password, so it is completely secure to use.

The Home-School Agreement

The Home-School Agreement might take many shapes, but it is essentially a 'contract' between you and your child's school about what you can expect from each other during the time she is there.

For some parents this agreement is merely stating the obvious and they would do the things asked of them and their child anyway, but for others it is a worthwhile document outlining the school's commitment to learning and care. For a few it might even be a useful prompt to organizing themselves and their children. It usually comprises:

1 A 'mission statement' of the school.

2 What the school expects from its teachers.

3 What the school expects from parents and children, especially with regard to absenteeism (holidays in particular), punctuality, behaviour, homework and uniform and/or the dress code – the latter a bit of an old chestnut.

If you or your child breaks the Home-School Agreement, you could be asked in to talk about it with the head teacher. In serious cases your child may be disciplined or excluded from school.

Special considerations

So far in this chapter we have explained the general principles to think about when choosing a school; however, for some children there are other considerations that will require particular thought.

Special needs

Your child will be offered tests for hearing and vision as part of normal post-birth health care, and it is essential that you attend these. If concerns arise during schooling about your child's progress or learning abilities, they will want to rule out hearing or visual problems first.

It can be rather worrying if you think that your child might have difficulty learning, but the incidence of special educational needs is much higher than most parents believe. The best way that you can help your child is to have an open mind and to collaborate with the school as soon as they think there is a problem.

It is far better that schools act sensitively to support children than leave them to struggle for too long. Let's take reading as an example. By the time your child is in Year 1, she should be able to decode simple texts such as picture books. If this is not the case then you shouldn't be unduly worried (there are many children who are late developers) but you would expect the school to have carefully assessed her and to have involved you in discussions about how you could help and what they will be doing to help at school.

For many children a slight change in the support they get will be enough to help them overcome the problem. However, if the problems are more difficult to solve, an Individual Education Plan might be drawn up. This is a plan of things that the school will do in addition to its normal work to specially support your child. Eventually, having gone through various stages of in-school support, some children will be given a Statement of Special Educational Needs, which will result in a much higher level of support, sometimes involving extra staff. (See Resources for more information on this.)

Bullying

If you suspect your child is experiencing repetitive instances of physical abuse or mental abuse by way of name-calling, you need to hear from her. If you are concerned, and if she hasn't said anything to you about it, ask her directly 'Is anyone hurting you at school?', then contact the school quickly and go in and talk to the headteacher and her class teacher about it. On the whole schools are pretty experienced and adept at resolving these issues.

early years

When does your child's education begin? Some might say it is in the nursery, at age three or thereabouts, but others would argue that it is from the moment a child is born. And the government seems to agree with that latter view, as its current education policy and initiatives are focusing very much on the provision for babies to five-year-olds, as well as providing support for parents and carers with babies, toddlers and very young children.

Every Child Matters

The Children Act 2004 paved the way for a new approach to transforming services for children from birth to age 19, through a programme called Every Child Matters: Change for Children. In the early years, as in other phases of education, this has resulted in a much more focused, regulated and goal-orientated programme. A key part of the approach is good-quality, free, early years provision for all three- and four-year-olds.

In educational jargon the new approach will be *multi-professional* and *interdisciplinary*. What that means to first-time parents is that learning is much more than just about schooling. For example, you can't learn if you're not healthy or if you're experiencing an abusive home background, so the new pre-school scenario takes in the 'whole picture', or another buzz word: the 'wraparound' approach.

A new raft of 'outcomes' with targets, and inspections for the wellbeing of children and young people from birth onwards (including educational achievement, obviously) has been set in motion. There are five outcomes which reflect universal ambitions, whatever a child's background or circumstances:

✪ Be healthy.

✪ Stay safe.

✪ Enjoy and achieve through learning.

✪ Make a positive contribution to society.
✪ Achieve economic wellbeing.

'Enjoy and achieve through learning' focuses on education and covers fundamentals such as getting children ready for school, ensuring that they attend and enjoy school (and recreation) and achieve national educational standards, as well as looking at personal and social development.

How Every Child Matters will affect you

Without a doubt the educational targets behind Every Child Matters are increasing the focus on the youngest children. This move is not without some controversy because many parents believe that this could put extra stress on the youngest children by setting targets that they are required to reach even before their first birthday.

Parental pre-school choices

With the goal posts for pre-school provision on the move, deciding on the best nursery or educational provision for your baby and toddler becomes even more of a minefield. In the light of these education changes how do you choose between a playgroup, a private day nursery, an early excellence centre, a kindergarten, a childminder, a maintained nursery school, a nursery class or a day nursery?

Early years options are far more varied than those for primary or secondary provision, but online sites can help tremendously to support your decision-making. Of course, what's suitable for your needs will most likely be affected by your personal and local circumstances – it can boil down to what provision best fits in with the working hours of the parents, in terms of when they can drop off and collect their child.

But within these constraints you do also need to think about who is providing the best quality of care and education for your child. This is why it is important to do a bit of research via the internet, including using local authority information, and also by talking to friends and neighbours (see page 55). A mixture of word-of-mouth, local information, as well as online research will help to inform your choice.

Choosing the right childcare at this age is, without a doubt, a big step for both you and your child, but there are many excellent online search tools to help you to find and research schools, childcare and early years settings – including Ofsted inspection reports (see pages 46–9). However, unlike primary and secondary schools, there are no league tables you can compare.

Visits with your child

Whatever provision you feel best suits you and your child (and that can be an instinctive decision), your choice should only be made after you have gathered as much information as you can and you have made a personal visit – with your child – to the pre-schools or childminders you have shortlisted. Why take your child? Well, this can give you a good insight as to how staff talk to him: listen as the staff talk to your child and observe his reaction.

Try to engineer a visit when there will be children there, so you can see if they are generally happy and engaged with their play and learning. Give yourself enough time to visit several possible options in your area to get a good idea of what could suit your child. Remember, there are lots of differences between the various types of childcare, early years or pre-school services, and also between individual childminders and early years staff. You can also ask for names of other parents to talk to about your chosen pre-school setting if you still have some doubts.

On-site visit checklist

1 Do the children seem generally happy and engaged?

2 Do the children play and talk together?

3 Are the staff talking to the children in a constructive way?

4 Are the staff friendly?

5 Are the staff interacting effectively with the children during their play?

6 Is there a good range of activities planned to help children learn and play? How often are these changed?

7 Is there a good range of well-maintained toys and equipment for children to use?

8 Are the premises clean, well-kept and safe for children; do they include a stimulating outside play area and are children taken to parks and other places regularly?

9 What kind of communication is there with parents?

10 What are the links with the local primary school?

Having gathered enough information you will ultimately need to trust your own gut feelings. Don't forget, who is the expert on your child? You.

Questions to ask

Cover these questions on your first visit, whoever the early care provider might be:

1 What qualifications do the staff hold?

2 What kind of ongoing training are staff involved in?

3 How many children do they care for?

4 What is the staff-child ratio?

5 What are the aims of the setting?

6 Can you look around the building to see the rooms?

7 Where do the children go to play outside?

8 Where will your child rest or sleep?

9 What kind of food and drink do they provide?

10 What are their healthy-eating guidelines?

11 How is a typical day organized?

12 How do they involve parents and keep them informed as to how their child is getting on?

13 Can you stay and join in at least two sessions to be sure this type of care is right for your child? Most early-years providers should be open to this suggestions and to talking freely to you about their ethos and your child.

14 Have all staff passed CRB (Criminal Records Bureau) checks? These are mandatory for anyone working with children, as are detailed background assessments.

Types of early years provision

The current provision for three- and four-year-olds varies considerably, with the state being the main provider in some areas and the private, voluntary and independent (PVI) sector dominating others.

All childminders and day-care providers – including playgroups, private nurseries, crèches and out-of-school clubs for under-eights – must be registered by Ofsted (or in Wales, by the Care Standards Inspectorate Bureau). Registration includes a criminal records check on anyone involved in providing childcare and an inspection of the premises to look at health and safety and educational welfare issues.

The registration certificate of the childcare provider should be displayed in the premises. If you can't see it, you should ask about this. The following explains most of the options for care and education for children from birth to five:

✪ **Crèches** provide occasional care for children under eight on particular premises on more than five days a year. Crèches need to be registered where they run for more than two hours a day, even where individual children attend for shorter periods. They are subject to national standards regarding supervisors, environment, safety, health, protection and documentation.

✪ **Toddler groups** are informal groups where parents and carers meet locally with their children on a regular basis – they are usually designed for children who are under five.

✪ **Nannies** provide childcare in your own home and can look after children of any age, as can au pairs to some extent. Most nannies have a recognized childcare qualification or nursery nurse training (but this isn't compulsory) and some are not inspected by Ofsted.

✪ **Childminders** do not all have childcare qualifications. However, anyone who is paid or rewarded in kind for looking after children under eight, for more than two hours daily on domestic premises, must register with Ofsted as a childminder. Ofsted will carry out periodic checks on the home and the childminder. What's more, all adults (16+) living and working in the childminder's home will be police- and health-checked. Some childminders will offer government-funded early education places for three- to four-year-olds; because they are providing both care and nursery education they are also subject to a special 'integrated inspection'.

Once you have met and interviewed a childminder you will get a feel for whether or not they are suitable for your child. A childminder is allowed to care for up to six children under the age of eight, including their own, but only three of them can be aged under five. Ask if they will agree to a trial run (say a couple of mornings) to see how it's going to work out. Most childminders should agree to this.

Childminders and your child's learning

You may think that the main role of a childminder is to provide care rather than education. In fact, they *are* expected to support your child's learning. The following quote from an inspection report in 2007 on a childminder in Hillingdon shows this:

The provision is outstanding. Children have great fun and play enthusiastically with an excellent range of toys and resources which fully promote their learning. The children make excellent progress because the childminder recognizes the uniqueness of each child. Close and caring relationships increase their trust and help them develop a strong sense of self. Children play with a wide range of appropriate toys and join in activities such as painting, cooking, sticking and playing imaginative games with play food.

Children display high levels of confidence in their daily activities and are developing very good independence skills, as they busy themselves and become absorbed in their

For parents looking for flexible care (perhaps because they work irregular hours that don't correspond to a normal 8am–6pm nursery day) such an arrangement could be ideal.

Home childcarers are another option; they are registered childminders who will work in your own home. If you choose this option you will need to register your home because you will be using it as a childcare setting.

Playgroups

Playgroups are very popular, so you need to get your child's name on the relevant list early. A playgroup is a group organized by the *activities. Their early communication skills are extremely well supported through high-quality interaction with the childminder. They play and explore their world at their own pace because the childminder has a secure understanding of how children learn. She gives them space to discover things for themselves but is always available to provide help or support when they need her.*

The children make positive relationships, they play exceptionally well together and are encouraged to consider younger children as they play.

The childminder offers children great opportunities to experience the wider world when they visit places of interest, for example, the library to change their books, the park, the swimming baths and when attending toddler groups. The children involve the childminder in their play and they receive an abundance of warm, individual attention that enables them to successfully extend their learning and experiences.

community, often by voluntary groups of parents, and usually runs on a not-for-profit basis. Sessions last from two-and-a-half hours to four hours a day, during term time, but not necessarily every day of the working week.

Most playgroups will provide places for between ten and 20 children. There should be one member of staff for every eight children aged three to five (this can rise to 1:13 if a qualified teacher is involved). Most staff will have qualifications to work with children or will be taking part in training.

One early years supervisor's take on how this system works is:

'We are preparing the children for big school and giving them the basic foundations of a general education which they will need at school – to get them ready to go to school, to help them to develop independence, to get social skills going, to work as part of a team and to be quite independent.'

Nursery classes, nursery schools and day nurseries

You can opt for state or private nursery classes and schools. Most day nurseries are privately run and some remain open during the school holidays. Most nurseries will take your child from the age of three until the point they join a reception class – which must be by the time they are five. More and more nurseries are also starting to take children younger than three.

Most children attend either five morning sessions or five afternoon sessions each week, although some types of nursery will offer part-time or full-time places, depending on your needs.

Nursery schools and classes have a minimum ratio of two adults to 20–26 children – one must be a qualified teacher, the other a qualified nursery assistant.

Nursery class as part of primary school

There are a number of advantages to placing your child in a nursery class that is part of a primary school: the nursery class must have a qualified teacher as the leader and there will also be nursery assistants with childcare qualifications.

If the nursery and the school that it is attached to are both good, the transition from nursery to reception class should be particularly smooth. Staff in this kind of nursery class will also be more aware of the demands that children face as they move up through the primary school.

Nursery school

A nursery school is one that only has children of nursery age, but they might have several classes. The advantage of a nursery school is that – in the good ones – the staff have great expertise about nursery children's needs. The slight disadvantage is that the links with local primary schools are not quite as strong as a nursery class that is part of a primary school. Staff in these nursery schools are therefore unlikely to have the same understanding of the structure of infant and junior years of local schools because they are not directly involved with them.

Private day nursery

Private day nurseries have more intensive staffing ratios and, depending on the ages of children being cared for, different rules on the qualifications of their staff from other part-time childcare providers. Day nurseries usually provide care for children from birth to five. Fees are charged for places in private day nurseries, but the government has a range of ways in which such fees can be offset, such as child tax credits and working tax credits. The National Day Nurseries Association offers information and advice for daycare providers and parents (see Resources for information).

Children's centres

Sure Start Children's Centres provide early education and full daycare for children under five, as well as a range of other services such as family support and health services. They provide integrated services and information from teams of professionals and are open a minimum of 10 hours a day, five days a week, 48 weeks a year. The Government is committed to delivering a Sure Start Children's Centre for every community by 2010. (See Resources for website address.)

Checklist for choosing a nursery

1 Does the setting have a recent Ofsted report you can see?

2 Does the nursery belong to a professional organization such as National Day Nurseries Association (NDNA), which keeps them informed of current issues?

3 Does the nursery have any Kite marks or awards of excellence?

4 Is there a safe and clean outside play area? If not, where are the children taken?

5 Is the interior bright, warm, clean and welcoming?

6 Is the equipment good-quality, clean, safe and appropriate?

7 Do they encourage healthy eating? How are meals/snacks organized and served?

8 Do the children in the nursery generally look happy and engaged?

9 Do the staff seem relaxed, well-presented and calm?

10 What is the staff-to-child ratio? The ideal is 1:3 for birth–two years; 1:4 for two–three years 1:8 for three–five years.

Assessing children's learning

The Early Years Foundation Stage (EYFS) brought together three previous frameworks in order to improve the coherence of provision for children from birth to five. All early years providers are required to use the EYFS to ensure that, whatever setting parents choose, they can be confident their child will receive a high quality learning experience that supports his development and learning.

Formal assessment of children learning at the foundation stage is based on the Early Years Foundation Stage Profile. This profile has 13 assessment scales, each of which has nine points of progression. The first three points represent early learning; the next five represent the kinds of things that children should

11 What are the staff qualifications? Half must hold relevant childcare qualifications, such as NVQ Childcare Level 2 or equivalent, and one should have a First Aid certificate. All supervisors require an NVQ Childcare Level 3 or equivalent.

12 How are parents kept informed about their child's activities and achievements?

13 Who will be your main contact and who will keep you informed? For example, will it be one named member of staff?

14 How much does it cost, and does that include nappies (if your child uses them), drinks and meals, holiday charges, and so on?

15 What's your gut feeling? Was your visit friendly, relaxed and informative? Did your child enjoy it?

16 Find out if your child's nursery has a programme to ease the transition to the reception class of a primary school. This is one aspect of good practice in a nursery.

be achieving by the time they finish in their early years setting; the final point represents achievement beyond what is normally expected.

You may find the thought of young children being assessed in this way to be somewhat mechanistic – and you wouldn't be the first person to argue this point! There is also the problem with the sheer number of statements that early years staff have to assess: do we want our children to begin having formal assessments of this kind so early in their lives? The acid test for you is whether the information that you are given by your child's early years setting is better because of this kind of structure, or worse. Either way, you need to be aware of the profile and ask for information about it.

Keeping an eye on your child in the early years

Nothing beats being with your child in their early days at nursery but, remember, early learning is also about encouraging a child's independence, so you (and the setting) have to balance you accompanying him on one or two visits with letting go so he won't get clingy and will get used to you NOT being around all the time.

The early years is certainly one of the phases where parents not only have the most daily contact with their child's learning, but also with other parents – who are all in the same boat for the first time. You will find that this is a good opportunity to swap news, views and comments, as well as to share experiences, which can be a tremendous boost to your confidence and make you feel secure in the knowledge that your child is getting the best start in his schooling.

Is your child happy?

The key question to ask once your child has started at his pre-school nursery, or in another sort of care, is: is he happy? Don't over-egg this point because a lot of children are naturally unsettled when they are first away from you – it's an emotional wrench for both sides – but as a rule of thumb your child should be happy to be going to nursery, or wherever. However, if he seems abnormally unhappy, he should be getting help from an identified member of staff, so keep an eye on the situation and monitor it, looking for positive and negative signs or nuances. If the situation persists you will need to go in and ask them about it; it is better to ask early and be reassured than to leave things too late. The way the setting handles your concerns will give you another little clue about the quality of the staff and organization.

A note on expectations

Remember, at the end of the day nursery education is – and should be – play-based: young children learn through play. However, the particular kinds of play, and the way that this play is organized, will make the difference between play that will accelerate children's learning and play that won't.

Because play is so important, many people are concerned about the disadvantages of 'too formal, too early'. Play is the natural way for children to learn and that is why you as a parent need to get involved with children's play at home to mirror what is going on at nursery.

Organizing play and activities that support learning in a nursery requires considerable skill and knowledge. Occasionally a lack of knowledge can result in low expectations on the part of nursery staff. For example, recent research has found that early years staff do not fully appreciate the sophisticated understanding of Information Technology that even very young children have. As with so much early years provision, striking the right balance between care, learning, play, fun and development requires careful handling.

The curriculum in the early years

The word 'curriculum' describes all the experiences that your child will encounter while learning. The curriculum for a nursery is decided by nursery staff who must take account of 'The Early Years Foundation Stage' curriculum.

There are six very broad areas of learning that every child has a right to learn, and these form the basis of the Foundation Stage curriculum. These are:

1   Personal, social and emotional development.

2   Communication, language and literacy.

3   Problem solving, reasoning and numeracy.

4   Knowledge and understanding of the world.

5   Physical development.

6   Creative development.

The Early Years Foundation Stage curriculum

Broadly speaking, teachers are given guidelines of what to expect from their very young pupils in terms of development and goals and what they should be encouraging them to do. As this book goes to press, current guidelines on the government's EYFS website (where video clips and other information is provided to explain these requirements – see Resources for website address) suggest that:

1 Personal, social and emotional development

Children must be provided with experiences and support which will help them to develop a positive sense of themselves and of others, respect for others, social skills, and a positive disposition to learn. Childcare providers must also look after their children's emotional wellbeing in order to help them to know themselves and what they can do.

2 Communication, language and literacy

Teachers need to encourage and promote children's learning and competence in communicating, speaking and listening, being read to and beginning to read and write. The children in their care must be provided with opportunity and encouragement to use their skills in a range of situations and for a range of purposes, and be supported in developing the confidence and disposition to do so.

3 Problem solving, reasoning and numeracy

Children need to be helped to develop their understanding of problem solving, reasoning and numeracy in a broad range of contexts in which they can explore, enjoy, learn, practise and talk about their developing understanding. In order to do this, children must be provided with opportunities in which they can practise and extend their skills in these areas and also to gain confidence and competence in using them.

4 Knowledge and understanding of the world

Children need to develop knowledge, skills and understanding that will help them to make sense of the world around them. Their learning needs to be supported by teachers offering them opportunities to use a range of tools safely; to come across creatures, people, plants and objects in their natural environments and in real-life situations; to undertake practical 'experiments', and also to work with a range of materials.

5 Physical development

The physical development of babies and young children must be encouraged by providing them with opportunities to be active and interactive and to improve their skills of coordination, control, manipulation and movement. Children of this age must be encouraged to use all of their senses to learn about the world around them and to make connections between new information and what they already know. They also need to be taught the importance of physical activity and making healthy food choices.

6 Creative development

Children need to be encouraged to be creative by being provided with support for their curiosity, exploration and play and opportunities to explore and share their thoughts, ideas and feelings, for example, through a variety of art, music, movement,

Different routes to starting school

		January
A September-born boy		3.3 years joins nursery class
An October-born girl with hearing impairment	Specialist teacher at home from age 6 months; from age two attends a local authority family centre two mornings a week	3.2 years continues to attend family centre two mornings a week
A December-born girl	Joins nursery centre soon after second birthday	3.0 years remains in nursery centre
A February-born boy with learning difficulties	Receives home teaching from age 1	2.10 years joins assessment unit in special school
A March-born boy	Cared for by childminder from age 9 months	2.9 years with childminder, plus visits to childminder's drop-in
A June-born girl		2.6 years at home and attends parent/toddler group
An August-born boy		2.4 years at home

September	September	September
3.11 years in nursery class	4.11 years joins reception class	5.11 years joins Year 1
3.10 years joins nursery school that has special unit	4.10 years remains in nursery school – joins reception class with support in summer term	5.10 years joins Year 1
3.8 years in nursery centre	4.8 years joins reception class – moves to mixed-age (reception and year 1) class in January	5.8 years remains in reception/ Year 1 class
3.6 years in special school nursery	4.6 years joins mainstream reception class	5.6 years joins Year 1
3.5 years remains with childminder who is now accredited as education provider; plus two mornings at pre-school	4.5 years joins reception class plus before- and after-school care with the same childminder	5.5 years joins Year 1
3.2 years joins independent school early years class	4.2 years remains in school early years class	5.2 years joins Year 1
3.0 years joins playgroup	4.0 years joins reception class	5.0 years joins Year 1

dance, imaginative and role-play activities, mathematics, and design and technology.

If you, as a parent, want to find out more about the curriculum at the EYFS and expectations for the birth to five-year-olds, visit the 'learning and development' section of the EYFS website (see Resources for website address).

Although your child does not legally have to start school until the term following their fifth birthday, in practice most children join a reception class in the September after their fourth birthday. There is considerable variation in the ages that children start in reception classes, as the chart on pages 90–1 shows.

primary school

Primary schooling is more straightforward than the complex early years options, which means that making a decision for this stage of your child's education will be simpler. So what do parents need to be aware of before they say 'goodbye' to their child and exit past the primary school gates?

A welcoming 'reception'

The reception class is the first class in a primary school; think of the word 'reception' as related to children being 'received' into the school. In the past, children would start in the reception class in the term of their fifth birthday (sometimes called 'rising fives'), and although this is still the case in some places, there has been a move towards children starting reception class at the beginning of the school year, regardless of when they are five. This means that most children will be four-year-olds when they start primary school.

The reception class is a time when the transition from the Early Years Foundation Stage (see Chapter 3) to the formal schooling of the National Curriculum in Year 1 is made. In the best reception classes, formal schooling does not start too early and so the transition is a smooth one. However, the government has increasingly encouraged more formal education at a younger age: the teaching of reading using synthetic phonics is an example of this. (The table on pages 90–1 illustrates some of the routes that children can take from the early years into a reception class.)

How does the National Curriculum kick in at primary level?

The National Curriculum Key Stage 1 covers children aged five to seven who are in Year 1 and Year 2 at primary school. Most parents still think of this stage as the formal, less play-based, start to their child's education, because this is where the National Curriculum

What is the National Curriculum?

The National Curriculum was first introduced following the Education Reform Act 1988 and aims to provide each and every child with access to a broad and balanced curriculum. (Although some argue that it simply re-introduced an educational code of some 100 years earlier, being a Victorian curriculum seeped in Victorian 'values'.)

Before this, teachers and children could follow topics that were interesting to them and had far more choice over their curriculum; now they have a much more rigid, test-orientated system and you and your child will have to be prepared for this. (You may also feel that this is a situation that, politically, you want to challenge at every opportunity!)

The National Curriculum begins in Year 1 and covers primary and secondary schooling up to the age of 16 – although reception class is designed to be a transitional stage from the Early Years Foundation Stage curriculum in to the National Curriculum. It includes attainment targets arranged in levels from one to eight (with an additional level for exceptional performance) for all the subjects in the curriculum. Expectations are laid down as to *what* children should have learnt and *by when*. This is the basis for the testing system, as the tests are intended to assess if a child has reached these levels of attainment set down in the National Curriculum.

kicks in and, at age seven, when children sit their first statutory tests (see page 101 for more information on these statutory tests).

Within the National Curriculum certain subjects are called 'core' subjects and as such are given more attention than the other 'foundation' subjects. Mathematics (maths for short), English and science are 'core' subjects, while others, including design and technology, geography and history, are 'foundation' subjects.

While maths and English are obviously vital as the stepping stones for so many other subjects, marking a distinction between core and foundation subjects has its negative side because it creates a two-tier curriculum, and who's to say that maths is more important than music, for example?

However, essentially, this division means that more time and resources are given to teaching, assessing and testing core subjects than foundation ones.

From Key Stage 1, every state school has to teach all these National Curriculum subjects:

1	English	Core
2	Mathematics	Core
3	Science	Core
4	Design and technology	Foundation
5	Information and communication technology (ICT)	Foundation
6	History	Foundation
7	Geography	Foundation
8	Art and design	Foundation
9	Music	Foundation
10	Physical education (PE)	Foundation

Modern foreign languages is not compulsory until Key Stage 3, although there are moves to introduce languages in primary school.

In addition to the subjects listed above, there is quite a complicated set of other requirements. Sex education is one of these, and so is the expectation of promoting spiritual, moral, social and cultural development throughout the National Curriculum. Schools also have to cover personal, social and health education (known as PSHE) and citizenship. Children have to develop key

Welcome to lessons in literacy and numeracy

The National Curriculum is the statutory part of the primary curriculum. Since 1997 the National Curriculum has been augmented by the literacy and numeracy strategies, which are now part of the Primary National Strategy – which is not statutory. The Primary National Strategy includes literacy and numeracy frameworks which specify in great detail the kind of teaching that should take place. (See Resources for more information.) These literacy and numeracy strategies have been controversial because they have taken government control of the curriculum to a very high level. Although they are non-statutory, great pressure has been brought to bear through the inspection system and the use of local authority consultants to hammer the messages home. It has taken courageous head teachers and teachers to try to use more imaginative and creative approaches to the curriculum, particularly if their school's statutory test scores are not above average. The result has been a rather dreary diet of daily one-hour lessons, although there are signs that this is finally starting to change.

skills, thinking skills and other skills. Religious education is another part of the curriculum which is somewhat different from the other subjects (see page 100). In primary schools, these subjects are not necessarily delivered in separate lessons; some teaching combines different subjects in themes or topics. For example, a history and geography topic might be 'our neighbourhood'. However, the National Curriculum does go through changes, for example, changes were made to the secondary school part of it in 2007.

All schools will ensure that their planning addresses the different subjects, but they won't necessarily present the material to the children by naming the subjects. This is because it is felt that children learn better when things are unified under one topic and connected by ideas and subject matter.

The 'REligion' word

Schools must provide RE (religious education) for all registered pupils as part of the National Curriculum, although parents can choose to withdraw their children from these classes on religious grounds if they wish.

All schools, other than voluntary-aided ones and those of a religious character, must teach religious education in a way that reflects the fact that the religious traditions in Britain are in the main Christian, while taking account of the teachings and practices of the other principal religions represented in this country.

Religious education is an important part of the school curriculum: not only does it develop a pupil's knowledge and understanding of religious beliefs and practices, and their influence on individuals, communities, societies and cultures, but it also enables pupils to consider their own spiritual development.

So religious education is covered by slightly different rules from other subjects. In the UK, the church has direct involvement in the funding of some schools and the claims that religious schools do better in the statutory tests has lead some to suggest that this proves that the influence of the church is a good one. However, such arguments rarely take into account the fact that church schools can select their pupils in different ways from schools funded only by the state. It's a tricky area, and it is one for personal parental choice. Your local authority will have separate statements about how religious education is covered, which you can find on their website or by visiting their offices. All of this raises the whole question of the influence of religion on England's education system (a topic for another book!), something that doesn't happen in other European countries.

The Statutory tests

At the age of seven, your child's teacher will assess her progress and attainment with the aim being to let you know how well she is progressing in relation to national expectations; to tell the subsequent school or teacher what she needs to learn next; and to gauge how well they, as a school, are teaching aspects of the National Curriculum.

Teacher Assessment goes on the whole time that your child is in school because it helps teachers to plan work that is appropriate to her learning needs, but it's especially important in her final year in Key Stage 1.

The Teacher Assessment covers:
- speaking and listening, reading and writing
- maths
- science

To help them make their assessments for English and maths, teachers use Key Stage 1 national tasks and tests. They must use enough tasks and tests to enable them to make a secure judgement. As a minimum, this will mean one test in each of:
- reading
- writing (including handwriting and spelling)
- maths

Schools have flexibility in the timing and range of the tasks and tests they use, and these can be administered at any time of their choosing to fit around other school work. All the tests added together last less than three hours. Teachers try to ensure that the children enjoy the experience, so they're able to do their best, but you can help your child by not making a big thing of it at home. The more relaxed you are, the better able she will be to tackle the test.

Why have targets and tests?

The context of how learning takes place is all-important, and ideally your child should gradually move from play-based learning to more teacher-directed activities.

The idea of tests and targets as part of this developing education does fill parents (and some teachers and educationalists) with dread because it is arguably an approach to learning that is narrowly results-orientated, rather than one designed to assess a child's all-round development. These tests can also exacerbate the 'too formal, too soon' problems. However, against that argument is the one that says that schools can use tests to check a child's progress, and so match their teaching to each child's needs and abilities.

We all know that children simply do not all make the same uniform progress, for example, some have special educational needs, so in a sense the tests are more a yardstick for the government to measure schools by rather than something that are helpful for you and your child.

Key Stage 1

The first target you'll come across at primary school is for seven-year-olds and is called 'Level 2'. Key Stage 1 has three levels (1–3) within which the great majority of pupils are expected to work, and Level 2 is the 'expected attainment' for most pupils at the end of this first Key Stage.

If your child finds her work easy, all well and good (although you may want to talk to her teacher about whether she should be aiming for a higher target), but if she is likely to find Level 2 a slog when she becomes seven years old, the school will tell you in good time. Remember, children develop at different rates. Some may not reach the set level at the given age, but they will catch up later. If your child needs extra help, a good school should be talking to you about how you can provide her with this. You will also hear your child's teacher talking about Level 2a, 2b or 2c; these are finer divisions of this second level for English and mathematics so that it is possible to differentiate between the attainment of different groups of pupils who achieve Level 2. Basically, 2a is high and 2c is low. These Level 2 tests are carried out by teachers and moderated by the local authority.

Key Stage 2

Key Stage 2 covers the school years 3, 4, 5 and 6. In Year 6 the summer term (and sometimes before) can be dominated in many classrooms by lots and lots of practices for tests. This support for children to get these tests right is because the government has put so much pressure on teachers and schools to achieve certain test results. The best thing you can do at this time is explain to your child that the tests are not particularly important; reassure her that it is good for her to do her best, but if she doesn't do too well it is not the end of the world. It really isn't necessary to do things like past papers at home; in fact this just increases the pressure. You should also be aware that some children do get very anxious about the tests and will need even more of your support.

Key Stage 2 has a range of 2–5 levels and the 'expected attainment' for most pupils at the end of this Key Stage (at age 11) is Level 4. If your child achieves Level 2c at age 7, she will have to work hard to reach Level 4 by the time she is 11.

Every school must give parents an annual report on how their child is progressing in each National Curriculum subject. The school is not obliged by law to give a level for each subject in this annual report, but some will.

At-a-glance checklist for your current school

		yes	no
1	Do you get regular reports about how your child is doing?	☐	☐
2	Is there a reading diary to fill in (for child and parent?)	☐	☐
3	Is the parent-teacher group active?	☐	☐
4	Are there worthwhile events organized to take the children out of school?	☐	☐
5	Is the dropping off/picking up process satisfactory?	☐	☐
6	Is the head teacher approachable when necessary?	☐	☐
7	Can you speak openly with your child's teacher?	☐	☐
8	Does your child receive positive feedback?	☐	☐
9	Of the food that is provided, are there healthy options?	☐	☐
10	Is the playground an interesting and suitable area for children to play in?	☐	☐
11	Does the school check visitors' entry?	☐	☐
12	Does your child get regular homework, but not too much?	☐	☐

So what can you do to help your child at primary school?

As you come to terms with the new learning regime of your child's primary schooling, just remember these three golden guidelines, which hopefully you have also used in pre-school and will continue to use in secondary school:

1 Take an interest in what your child is learning at school.
2 Encourage her to tell you about it.
3 Praise her when she has done well.

This is fine as a general guide, but how else can you help your child at her new school at a simple, practical level?

Preparing them for a new primary school

In the early days of being at her new school, you might find that your child needs a little more of your time and support than usual, until she gets settled into the new routine. So, help her by:

❂ Being a good listener. Listen and respond to what she tells you.

❂ Encouraging her to ask questions and explain that it's good to do that at school, too.

❂ Ensuring the morning routine prepares her for the school day.

❂ Meeting with other mums or dads and her friends en route to class during the first days and weeks.

Preparing them for prep: how to help with homework

Homework is another sign that your child has progressed from learning through play to formal education, and this is the time that you need to up the ante on support for her.

The reading book

At the start of primary schooling, the most common form of homework will be the reading book that your child brings home. This could be a real book (a 'trade' book that is available in most bookshops) or a reading scheme book, or even one of each. Alongside this she will also be given a reading diary/observation book which you, the parent, need to, at the very least, sign to say that you have shared the book with your child. Better still, you could add a comment in the designated column about how well, or otherwise, your child got on with a particular book.

It's really important that you engage with this process – you need to sit down with your child and share the book with her and read together. (For more advice and suggestions on how to do this, see *How to help your child read and write* – see Resources for more information on this title.)

Checklist for helping with spelling homework

1 Go through her homework and encourage her with it. Work with her and help her through the spellings.

2 Use the *look-cover-write-check* (or similar method): this involves you looking at the word together, before the child or parent covers the word with their finger, then the child tries to write the spelling, and finally the word is revealed and checked.

3 Remember the physical act of writing is hard work – so don't hurry her.

4 Occasionally, try using home-made flash cards to inspire her to write down words.

5 Encourage your child to use letter names when talking about letters. Also talk about the sounds that letters make in words.

6 An important consideration is the meaning of the words – make sure your child understands what they mean because that will also help her remember them. Bear, bare: you can't spell them write (right!) unless you know which meaning you're talking about.

7 Use word games such as i-spy for younger children, Boggle®, Scrabble®, hangman, and the like.

Spelling tests

As your child progresses through the first couple of years of primary school and into Year 2, the next thing you will encounter is a steady stream of spelling lists, leading into Statutory tests beginning at around age 7 – Key Stage 1.

Again, the most important thing that you can do here is to be actively involved. So, make sure you keep the spelling sheet in a safe place – preferably a homework place for your child; be clear

A spelling scenario: a helping hand

Every week Jack had his spelling to do, which was becoming a bit repetitive and boring. Jack's dad had spiced it up with games of scrabble, and it was while playing this that Dad put down the word 'Qadi' ['*qadi': Islam, cadi a magistrate in Muslim countries*].

One day during weekly spelling practice Jack told his teacher, but she insisted that there were no words beginning with 'q' that don't have a 'u' after it. Undeterred, Jack spoke to his dad and they looked in a dictionary together. Back at school, clutching a photocopy of the dictionary page, Jack told his teacher. To her credit, she gave Jack a house point but then added, 'It's not really an English word, though, is it?'.

This scenario tells us a little about the English language and the teacher's approach to learning. In fact, there are quite a few words beginning with 'q' which are not followed by a 'u', such as 'qwerty' and 'Qatar', to mention just two.

The key point is that if a word appears in a standard English dictionary then it is an English word (although it may have originally come from another language). So this is a very good reason for owning an up-to-date, high-quality dictionary such as Chambers, Longman's, Oxford, and so on.

The teacher's praise of Jack for his discovery was good, but she should have thought to say to Jack, 'That's really interesting, I didn't think there were any words like that. Let's have a look in a dictionary. She should also understand about the ways in which English words enter the language.

Checklist for helping with homework

1 Create time for your child to do her homework and try to ensure it is when you can be around to offer support.

2 Make homework a regular part of the daily routine, say 30 minutes after a meal followed by one hour of play before bedtime, or perhaps straight after school before she relaxes into being back at home.

3 Create a space for homework; avoid competing activities and distractions, especially from other family members, pets, and so on.

4 Make homework time a positive and fun experience. Be enthusiastic, offer her a drink, give help, mediate online materials by working together and suggest relevant books.

5 Homework should be more varied but, sadly, the dominance

when the deadline for learning the spellings is; test your child's memory for the words (but try to keep this fun); make sure that she understands the meanings of the words, as well as memorizing their spellings; and play word games to help her spelling on a more general level.

Helping with topic-based homework and projects

In Key Stage 2, probably in Year 5 or Year 6, you will also start to encounter broader topic-based homework, such as covering the Vikings or Victorians in history classes. Here you have tremendous scope as a parent to encourage and steer your child on her learning quest. The most helpful ways are by:

- ✪ Books (your own or a visit to the library).
- ✪ Trips to a museum or local site.
- ✪ Searching the internet together.

of maths and English has narrowed the choice, so it's often left to parents to give their child a broader range of experiences in say, music, foreign languages or certain sports.

6 To encourage maths learning at home, try games and puzzles you can do together with numbers. Simple dice or snakes-and-ladders or moving-around-the-board games will help her to count, as will physical games such as What's the time, Mr Wolf? (for example, 3 o'clock = 3 steps, and so on).

7 Maths is not just about sums, but it also involves measuring, shapes and spaces, so cooking is an absolute gift for teaching your child maths. You can use ingredients, measuring scales and measuring jugs to help her to learn about numbers.

Often the homework given to your child on these topics will allow her some choice. Your child will be invited to choose a subject within a framework, but you need to make sure that she understands how and what to search for when she is researching it on the internet and, critically, how she can 'translate' the often difficultly worded information into her own words.

And that's the key to this whole process: she has to understand the subject – it's no good her just copying information and doing a cut'n'paste job.

The whole process of accessing suitable sites via the internet – which keywords, which search engine you use – is a potential minefield. You are literally bombarded with millions of sites, so how do you know which ones to go for? If in doubt, choose those with reputable names that you already trust, such as the BBC, the British Museum, National Geographic, or similar such specialist institutions that are child-friendly.

Libraries/mobile libraries/online library help

The inaccuracies on some websites raises the question of how much we can really rely on the internet to give us the right information, and I would argue that a good selection of reference books is still a very important source of information.

In these modern, technologically dependent times, don't forget how good books are. Remember, too, how helpful a librarian can be; it's really important to take a child to the library regularly

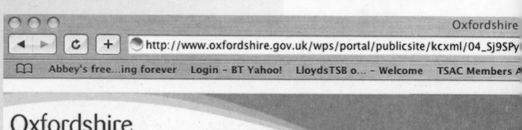

Oxfordshire

http://www.oxfordshire.gov.uk/wps/portal/publicsite/kcxml/04_Sj9SPy

Abbey's free...ing forever   Login – BT Yahoo!   LloydsTSB o... – Welcome   TSAC Members A

Oxfordshire
All you need to know about Oxfordshire from your county council

| Home | Council services | News | About Oxfordshire | Contact us |

LOCATION: Home > Council services > Leisure and culture > Libraries > Library services

- ⌃ Council services
- ⌃ Leisure and culture
- ⌃ Libraries
- ❯ **Library services**
- ■ Information links
- ■ Newspapers and magazines
- ■ Activities and events
- ■ Borrowing services
- ■ Business Information Point
- ■ In the library
- ■ Local and family history
- ■ Reading groups
- ■ **Reference online**

Reference online

Oxfordshire Libraries can now offer all our members access to a wid

If you are using an Oxfordshire library computer click here for

We are delighted to offer this extended access to our reference an year.

You will need to enter your library membership number after clickin

Britannica Online (Library Edition)

Access: Britannica Online

Grove Art Online

Access: Grove Art Online
N.B. *Enter L followed by your library membership number.*

Grove Music Online

Access: Grove Music Online
N.B. *Enter L followed by your library membership number.*

News UK

Oxfordshire's grisly past

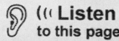

(((**Listen**
to this page

because librarians are trained to help your child find the right books and other sources of information.

Libraries can also be accessed online, and if you have a library card you can tap in your number to access fantastically reliable sources, such as Oxford Reference Online or the Encyclopedia Britannica – which you would otherwise have to pay for.

Here's an online library example:

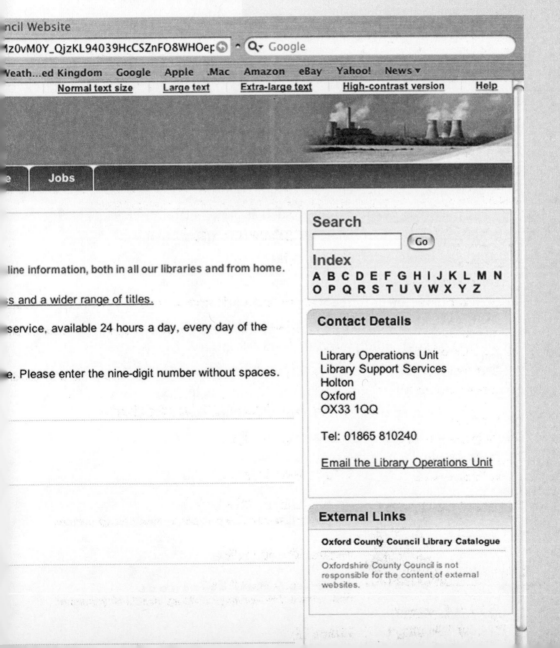

You also need to help your child understand that some websites are more reliable than others when researching homework, so try to find a minimum of two sites on the same topic and compare their information. You will no doubt have heard of Wikipedia, for example, the online encyclopedia. Wikipedia's information is provided by its users, and these contributors vary a great deal in their expertise. One of the good features of this site is that the users who provide information have to keep arguing about information until they agree, a process which can help improve its reliability. The down side is that they may not know a great deal about the topic. This is a very different way of gathering information from the traditional methods by which, say, an expert will compile a book which will go through several checks to ensure its accuracy.

Such sites, and the web generally, are often quite adult-orientated and frequently above primary level understanding. One way round this is to go to child-orientated sites, such as CBBC, or children's search engines, such as Yahooligans, or check the 'Kids' icon on mainstream sites. Again, this doesn't in itself guarantee total reliability, so your child should not simply download and cut'n'paste. If she hasn't really read it and re-worked the information in her own words, will she have understood it?

As a parent you need to consider whether you want to place restrictions on your child's internet access. It is very easy to come across inappropriate material when searching for something. If you are concerned about what material your child is being exposed to, go to the preferences area of your browser where you can adjust security settings according to your needs. If in doubt, contact your service provider for more information.

Extra tuition?

If you feel your child is really struggling with core subjects as she approaches the Key Stage 2, Year 6 tests, you might also consider the possibility of extra private tuition. Yes, it smacks of pressure and targets, but the number of private maths and English tuition ads suggests there is a healthy market for this kind of help, and you'll have to dip into your pocket.

Nevertheless, good private tuition (though hard to find) can really help to stimulate your child's learning, while a one-on-one hour a week can be a great confidence boost for both child and parent. To find such help, check your local ads, talk to other parents and don't be afraid to ask your child's teacher (he will know who is on the grapevine).

Activities outside school: local events

Keep an eye open for events in your nearest city, such as science weeks or children's literature festivals. These and other events are often put on by local museums or galleries and will be advertised in your local paper, as well as in the local library. They are a worthwhile trip out, as they can really help to stimulate your child's learning and, indeed, directly help a project, topic or specific curriculum-related subject. The same goes for music or sports events; there are more than likely to be things happening at the local leisure and sports centre, but enrol your children quickly as classes can get heavily oversubscribed.

Teacher

If in doubt about how you can help your child, one of the first things you can do is ask your child's new primary class teacher. Not only can this give you much-needed confidence that you are doing the right thing, but it can also help to build a bond or relationship with that teacher.

Internet

The other useful aid is the internet. This has really come into its own and there are plenty of well-thought-through government-sponsored and commercial sites that will give you the lowdown on *what* will happen to your child and *when*; how you can support her; what to expect at different stages of schooling; reference and help to download on test and topic-based projects; special needs and lots more. A full list of resources is given at the end of this book.

The Department for Children, Schools and Families and the Qualifications and Curriculum Authority also have a number of subject-specific leaflets to help parents in understanding the National Curriculum, and more information is also available from the sites teachernet and curriculum online. The Help Your Child Discover... series of leaflets (available from the parents centre section of the DCSF website – see Resources for all these website addresses) has been designed to support you in helping your child with her school work.

Parents' evenings and reports

In Chapter 2 we explained the importance of having a helpful attitude towards parents' evenings. Most primary schools now hold at least two parents evenings per academic year. The first one is particularly important because you can find out what you can do to help your child during her school year, and then there will also be another one later in the year which will be more concerned about what your child has achieved.

In the final term of each year you will also receive a report about your child. This will give you some information about National Curriculum levels and about different subjects. Unfortunately, some of this can be a bit bland, but the best reports should tell you something constructive about your child in language that is meaningful. When this happens you are more likely to talk to your child about some of her memorable achievements which are mentioned in the report, which in turn adds another layer to her learning as she remembers what she did.

Last, but certainly not least, the basic worry: is your child happy?

Ask most parents what they want for their child at school and they will say 'to be happy'. So what does that mean?

This is more than just asking her directly, 'are you happy?', it's about being aware of your child's moods and chatting with her about the things she does at school. Don't forget to ask her what she does at playtimes as well as during lesson time; happy children will tend to get on reasonably well with their peers and have some close friends.

If your child is happy and thriving at school you would expect her to be:

1 Happy to be going to school in the morning.
2 Tired, but happy to see you after school.
3 Motivated about school.

It can be quite tricky to work out why your child is demotivated: it could be that she doesn't particularly like her teacher, or it could be a particular thing that is happening in class (if so, you need to discuss this with her teacher). Sometimes it will be a product of the country's curriculum and testing system which can make school boring. This is not something that you can change overnight, but it is something that you can influence if you put forward your views at appropriate moments, even when just talking to other parents.

If your child is not happy, arrange to see the teacher first and discuss the evidence for your conclusion (including what she herself has said that makes you think this), and share this with the teacher to discover his take or perspective on it.

If you feel your child is not making friends then there are things that the teacher can do to help. One of the simplest things that you can do is to encourage your child to invite someone from the class to come round to your house to play or to have tea.

secondary school 11–16

With your child entering secondary school as a pre-teen rising to a fully fledged teenager – hormones kicking in, challenging authority, testing the boundaries of acceptable behaviour, and so on – you may well have quite a lot on your plate in helping your child at school, as well as at home. Challenging behaviour that your child exhibits at home is a natural part of growing up in a 'safe' environment. But if too much of this kind of behaviour is happening at school, this can create problems for you and your child. The last thing you need is suddenly to be contacted by letter about, say, your child's unruly behaviour, unreported absences or unsubmitted homework.

There is a raft of issues that a parent will have to contend with when their child starts and moves through the various stages of secondary school, and in order to address them it is best to break them down into manageable chunks.

1 Moving on up: the transition from primary to secondary school.
2 Finding the right school.
3 The first years of secondary school: teaching and assessing.
4 Helping with homework and supporting study.
5 The later years at secondary school: choices and options for GCSEs.
6 Troubleshooting when things go wrong.

Moving on up

The primary-secondary transition is quite different from that of pre-school to primary changeover, because children of 11 years of age are much more independently minded. This can be a mixed blessing: on the one hand they are potentially ready to be stimulated by a much bigger and more diverse establishment (with not just one but many teachers to interact with), but on the flip side they are also less willing to be told what to do by figures of authority. At home you will discover that 'Keep Out' signs on the bedroom door are starting to mean what they say, and mobile phone texting and internet chatrooms open up worlds that are difficult for a concerned parent to monitor.

But growing up and being independent are not things that happen overnight, and children entering secondary school will still experience some of the reactions to their new environment that four- and five-year-olds do when they go into reception class. In fact, just finding their way around an enormous set of school buildings – which is what most secondary establishments are – and moving along the endless corridors to different classrooms and orientating themselves takes some doing.

Without any doubt, the transition from primary to secondary is a big leap and quite a daunting, possibly unsettling, challenge. And that's precisely where the new school should be helping your child.

The shock of the new

Both the Government and secondary schools themselves have woken up to the fact that parents and children need help coping with the scale of the move from primary school into secondary education. After all, a child might be moving from a village primary of 120 pupils to a suburban secondary with over 2,000 pupils.

Talk to other parents who have children who are just starting at secondary school and many will tell you how their 'little ones' at primary – even though they were in the eldest class – seem so tiny and vulnerable in the new environment of such a massive school. From being the 'biggest fish in a small pond' they suddenly seem like minnows in a big sea; 'Now she's at secondary school she's having to grow up fast', is a typical response.

Coping badly with the new: Connie's story

'It was scary at first because I didn't know anybody and it was such a big place compared to primary school where I knew everyone. I was also scared about getting detention because you never got that kind of thing at primary school. And generally I felt frightened because you don't know what is going to happen. It took me about four weeks to settle down.'

CONNIE, 12 YEARS OLD

Connie didn't seem to be getting any in-school support. Ideally, she should have already visited her designated or 'feeder' secondary school as part of organized Year 6 visits with her primary teacher. That's 'best practice' while children are still in final year of primary; it allows them not only to have an early experience of the new establishment, but also to have a fun day with a bit of learning too. They will also get a feel for the place, as this example shows:

Coping well with the new: Jack's story

'Our class spent two days in a row at the next school we would be going to. We went on the secondary school bus with the older children. I got to know my class teacher. When we arrived we were mixed in with other primary schools and then the teacher told us which forms we'd be in. I was a bit nervy because you're leaving your primary school, but the visits were fun and exciting. We were shown round other bits of the school by a Sixth form boy and girl – then we had a feedback session at our primary school with our teacher doing questions and answers.'

A good secondary school will have a well-thought-through plan for helping primary children not only before, but also once they arrive

Extra targeted help for the big move

Recognizing the big hike in academic demands from primary to secondary level, the government are seeking to ensure extra support for 11-year-olds in order to help them have a smooth transition between schools. Some children may be helped by 'booster' programmes in Year 6.

Booster programmes are for those pupils who need extra, targeted support to achieve Level 4 in their statutory tests. The majority of schools target small groups of around 6 to 15 pupils, depending on the size of the Year 6 cohort. The DCSF (Department for Children, Schools and Families) thinks that it is a good idea that these happen outside school hours, possibly even at weekends. However, you might think that the pressure of the statutory tests is quite enough in-school without more spilling over into the children's own time! There may also be literacy and numeracy summer schools available in the summer holiday before they start Year 7.

For those pupils who need additional support in Year 7, catch-up programmes have been developed. In mathematics, the Springboard 7 programme consolidates what your child has learnt in Year 6 and leads him smoothly into Year 7. In English, half-term literacy progress units are available for pupils experiencing difficulty with certain aspects of reading and writing.

Like so many things in education, these programmes are designed in part to boost children's test performance. As a parent you will have to weigh up whether a summer school is likely to be as good for your child's learning as the time that they could be spending with their family and friends.

to start their first term. For example, this might include a scheme whereby the whole school doesn't start on the same new term date. This enables Year 7s to have some time at the school with fewer pupils around. They have the chance to settle in before the rest of school begins, and can get used to their new surroundings so they don't find them too intimidating.

Another good scheme is the buddy system (especially for a child who has switched schools mid-term) where the child is given a buddy to help him orientate and 'show him the ropes'.

Some schools will also ask the new intake to nominate in advance close friends from their primary school that they would like to be in the same form with. This might be a list of several children that includes one or two in particular who are their close friends.

New challenges

It's fair to say that many Year 6 children will have outgrown their primary school and will be ready to be challenged by teachers with more in-depth subject knowledge in the separate subjects taught at secondary school. Of course, they will also have to hit it off with a wider range of teachers than they have been used to.

Other children may have had a really good experience with their primary teacher in Year 6, if, say, she allowed them a fair degree of independence, so it can be a big wrench perhaps to find that their secondary school initially seems rather 'back to basics'. Before the statutory tests were introduced, Year 6 used to be a time when children were offered high levels of independence. They were able to pursue topics in-depth that were of real interest to them.

Supporting the child as he settles into the new school

As a parent you need to be especially sensitive to your child's needs in this transition phase and it helps if you ask him about:

○ how it's going

✪ the new things he is experiencing

✪ the ways in which you can help

✪ things he wants to talk to you about

Finding the right school

When it comes to choosing the right school for your child there are a few considerations you need to be aware of. If your child will be going to a state school, travel must be a key consideration. How far will he have to go? Will it be on foot, by bike, by bus or car?

At-a-glance checklist for your new secondary school

	yes	no
1 Does the school have a plan to help the new intake settle in?	☐	☐
2 Does it have a 'buddy system' to help the new pupil?	☐	☐
3 Do you know where and when the school bus leaves?	☐	☐
4 Can your child walk safely to school or the school bus stop?	☐	☐
5 If you are not close to the school, do you have a school run or alternative bus route sorted?	☐	☐
6 Has your child completed a 'safer cycling course' at his primary school?	☐	☐
7 Do you know the times of morning registration/assembly?	☐	☐
8 Have you got all-important school names and phone numbers to hand? Has the school got all your contact numbers?	☐	☐
9 If your child is having a lunch box, who'll be making it?	☐	☐
10 Does the school have a healthy-eating canteen?	☐	☐
11 Have you got a morning routine sorted out?	☐	☐
12 Have you got a routine for your child coming home? Are one or both of you working?	☐	☐

You need to weigh up how he will get there against what the school has to offer, and this could mean making a crude choice between the nearest school or, if the local school is not as good as it should be, a better school.

At the beginning of the autumn term, possibly in September, your child will bring home a letter and some information about choosing a secondary school. An application indicating your preferred choice of secondary school is usually required from October onwards (local authorities have very useful online timetables to ensure you don't miss key dates). If you prefer, you can complete an online application, but late applications have to be done in writing. Information about how to find your local authority and make an application online is available on the directgov website. In the spring term the local authority will write to you to inform you about the school that your child has been allocated to. There is an appeals system if your child is not placed in the school of your choice but, once again, it works to strict dates that you need to be aware of.

There is likely to be more than one secondary school in your catchment area, so you may decide, for a variety of reasons, that

Earlier chapters of this book have referred to examples of Ofsted reports for early years and primary settings. Most of the features for secondary school Ofsted reports are similar, however, one of the main differences is that secondary schools are much bigger and are organized into subject departments. They also frequently specialize in particular areas of the curriculum. You may find that some areas of the curriculum and provision are of more interest to you and your child than others, so you should look at these aspects in the reports particularly carefully.

you want to take advantage of the wider choice and look at all the options before you select a school. If that is the case you need to:

✪ Check the options with the local authority (offices or website).

✪ Check school websites and download prospectuses, or order them from the schools if you prefer.

✪ Arrange to visit the schools.

✪ Check the Ofsted school reports.

✪ Assess test/exam information, such as the Secondary School Performance Tables which are provided online by the Department for Children, Schools and Families (see Resources for website address).

League tables

The Department for Children, Schools and Families produces achievement and attainment tables (formerly performance tables or league tables) which show how well schools do in exams and tests. These online tables, also printed periodically in the national and local press, can show you the achievements of pupils in secondary schools and how they compare with other schools in your area, and across England as a whole.

There are over 4,500 secondary schools in England alone, so the tables can seem like you are wading through a jungle. Among the point-scoring statistics you can find information on:

✪ The Key Stage 3 results of pupils in English, mathematics and science, which will highlight those schools whose pupils mostly fall below Level 5, or those who exceed that level.

✪ The GCSE/GNVQ achievements of school-leaving-age pupils.

✪ Rates of pupil absence from school – both with permission and without.

✪ 'Contextual value-added' (CVA) assessments. This enables comparisons to be made between schools with different pupil intakes. It's a way of measuring the progress that individual pupils have made between taking statutory assessment tests at age 7, 11,

14 and 16. (For an at-a-glance table of how 'years' relate to age and Key Stages see page 16.) So school A might show high percentages of pupils achieving Level 5 and above, while school B shows lower percentages. But in 'CVA' terms, the pupils at school B may have made more progress than other pupils who were performing at the same level at Key Stage 2, and therefore the school will have a higher value-added 'score' than school A. The Contextual value-added assessment is designed to meet concerns that the calculation does not account for schools serving the most difficult or deprived catchments.

However, remember that these tables provide only part of the picture of each school's overall achievements. You also need to consider all of those alongside the other important sources of information already mentioned above, such as Ofsted reports, admission criteria and local knowledge about the area that they serve. (See Resources for DCSF and Ofsted websites for more information on this.)

The first years of secondary: teaching and assessing

Lessons and learning

The main difference between the teaching and learning in your child's last class in the primary school and the classes at secondary school is the move from having predominantly one teacher for all lessons at primary school to having different teachers for each subject at secondary school.

The advantage of this is that each secondary school teacher has a greater knowledge about his or her subject, which enables him or her to extend your child's learning to higher levels.

The disadvantage is that it is more difficult for teachers to form meaningful social relationships with their pupils because they see them less often.

Some schools will try to make this change easier for pupils by organizing the Year 7 curriculum to reflect some aspects of the primary school, which can be very beneficial indeed.

During their first year at secondary school (Year 7), pupils will be assessed periodically during their lessons. They will also probably have end-of-year assessments. The important thing to bear in mind about these assessments is that they will contribute to the subject 'ability' groups, or 'sets', that your child will be put in during Year 8. You should also be aware of the fact that some secondary schools may pitch their teaching at a level which is too low for some children; this is because some teachers mistakenly feel the need to 'go back to basics' with Year 7 pupils. In good secondary schools teachers will take into account the assessment information they are given by the primary school and build their teaching on this. If at any time in their schooling your child feels that the work is too easy, you should make an appointment to see a teacher. At secondary school this will be the form teacher or the head of year.

Ability grouping

Ability grouping is the practice of putting pupils into different groups based on their perceived abilities. There has been considerable debate about whether ability grouping is good for pupils' learning or not. Research has shown both positive and considerable negative effects.

Typically, during Year 7, schools don't group by ability; instead they tend to start teaching pupils in form groups of mixed ability. How schools plan their groups and allocate pupils to specific groups can often be a bit of mystery to parents. If schools choose to use ability groups (and currently most do from Year 8 onwards) then the process of allocating pupils to groups must be transparent and fair. There are a few key principles behind this:

1 Allocation to different groups should be based on rigorous analysis of assessments.

2 The level of work in class should stretch but not frustrate your child. It should also be genuinely different in each of the various ability groups.

3 Assessments should be carried out at least three times a year.

4 Pupils should be able to move group mid-year.

5 Nothing should stop pupils who achieve the necessary assessment outcomes from moving to a higher group.

In reality, other factors are likely to play a part. One of the most difficult ones is the fact that class sizes are restricted to what is manageable in the space allocated for each classroom. In addition, it is argued that class sizes need to be equitable so that all teachers are teaching roughly the same number of pupils in each class.

As a parent you should try to find out how and when these decisions are made and ensure that your child understands what is happening. It can also help if you share information about your child's interests at home that might have a positive bearing on their work in different subjects. It is possible that this information might beneficially influence an overall decision about which group your child will end up in.

The downside to all this is that subject sets can become a disincentive if your child feels he's never going to be moved to another set. If your child is in the bottom set there may also be a low expectation from some teachers which can have a damaging effect on his self-esteem, especially if he is in the lowest sets for all subjects and sees little chance of 'escaping'.

So it's not just the parents, but also the pupils who need to know and be empowered as to how their school's systems work.

In general, schools tend to be very bad in briefing on how their ability groupings work; you have to prise out the information. The key thing is that the child should feel that the level of work he is given is appropriate for him, meaning that it is stretching him enough and is neither too easy nor too difficult.

What are subject sets?

So you've heard the term 'subject sets' being bandied about, but you might be thinking, 'What are they?'

The most common subject sets you will come across are where pupils are, as the name suggests, grouped into different classes by subject on the basis of their scores in assessments. For example, there might be three English sets: set 1, set 2 and set 3 (where 1 is the top, 2 the middle and 3 the bottom set).

Sets become more and more important as your child progresses through his secondary school because ultimately they will decide whether your child will be entered for higher or lower GCSEs. Crudely put, it means a low-set class won't be entered for, say, English GCSE Grade A or B because the pupils in it would not be expected to achieve that grade.

What is streaming?

Streaming is where pupils have *all* their subjects in a particular class, which is grouped by ability. No differentiation is made between subjects in this situation, which makes it a rather closed notion that suggests children have a fixed ability, rather like an IQ (intelligence quotient). The idea that a child has a fixed level of intelligence runs the risk of denying what they might achieve in future. As a result of its controversial nature, streaming is not very common.

Although schools try hard to make allocation to sets fair, this is not a purely mathematical process, so judgements have to be made. It is worth asking why your child is in a particular set (there's no need for schools to withhold that information) and you should discuss this with the teachers to make sure there is a good reason for their decision.

It's important to discuss this aspect of learning with your child. Ask him where he wants to be. He might not be happy in a top set because it is too pressurized, or he might feel that his set is at too low a level. Armed with this information, you could ask the school or a specific subject teacher how they've determined your child's sets.

Key Stage 3 targets, tests and assessments

Key Stage 3 (KS3 for short) stands for the first three years of secondary education when your child is between 11 and 14 years old. These are vital years: it's a time when your child develops the knowledge and the skills that he needs for his future education.

From the ages of 13 to 14 your child will work towards important Year 9 statutory tests in English, maths and science that often have a bearing on the levels of GCSEs that he will ultimately sit. (See page 52 for information on statutory tests.)

The tests cover:

1 English (including reading, writing and studying a Shakespeare play)

2 Maths (including mental maths)

3 Science

The tests are taken during one week at the beginning of May. When added together, all the tests last about seven or eight hours. Your child won't be tested on anything that hasn't been covered by the National Curriculum and the test papers are sent to an external marker to be marked. Technically, children do not pass or fail these tests their results are simply given as a level.

As well as the test results, your child's strengths and weaknesses in English, maths and science are also monitored, evaluated and summed up in a 'teacher assessment', the teachers' professional judgement on what level your child is working at.

Teacher assessments for 14-year-olds

Teachers will also monitor your child's progress in all National Curriculum subjects and provide an assessment for these subjects:

1 English
2 Maths
3 Science
4 History
5 Geography
6 Modern foreign languages
7 Design and technology
8 Information and communication technology (ICT)
9 Art and design
10 Music
11 Physical education
12 Citizenship
13 Religious education

Levels 5 and 6

For both the tests and teacher assessments your school will send you a report telling you which National Curriculum levels your child attained. The full range of teacher assessment levels that can be awarded is from W (Working towards a Level 1) to 8. Remember, as a yardstick, at the age of 14 most children are expected to achieve Level 5; many will also be expected to achieve Level 6. A minority of pupils will reach Level 7 or above.

As has already been highlighted, children develop at different rates and some children will find their work easy, while others won't. If your child is not being stretched, talk to his teacher about aiming for a higher target. If your child is likely to find Level 5 hard when he gets to age 14, the school should tell you in good time. In this situation your child may need extra help from his school and from you, so talk to his teacher about how you can help. (See page 135 for an example of a school report showing attainment levels.)

Helping with homework and supporting study

Within a few weeks of starting secondary school, pupils will get homework (and quite a lot of it) every night. Government guidelines recommend that secondary-school children should be given the following amount of homework:

Years 7 and 8 (age 11–14):   45–90 minutes per day
Year 9 (age 14):   1–2 hours per day
Years 10 and 11 (age 15–16):   1.5–2.5 hours per day

When should you offer help with homework?

Children can feel quite daunted by this increased amount of homework, as it is a big step up from what they were used to at primary school. Homework at this level will also be more varied than it was at primary school, and as a parent you will find that the greatest change for you is that increasingly you may not be able to help with homework tasks because you don't have the up-to-date knowledge of the subject that your child has. You may also find that your input is just not wanted!

This is not such a bad situation: children need to become

TWICKENHAM SCHOOL

YEAR 9 ACADEMIC PROGRESS MONITORING REPORT

Emily Hunt 9JW

SUBJECT	ATTAINMENT LEVEL	CAUSE FOR CONCERN	EFFORT	TEACHER
English	5a		B	Miss L. Jordan
Mathematics	6c		B	Mr J. Foley
Science	7c		A	Mr N. Andrews
German	4a	b	C	Ms B. Scott
D & T	6a		B	Mr D. Knox
ICT	6a		A	Mr A. Skinner
Geography	6c		C	Ms C. David
History	6c		B	Mrs B. Million
R.E.	5c		B	Ms L. Bower
Art	5a		A	Mrs A. Collier
Drama	5a		B	Ms C. O'Brien
Music	6b		A	Mr M. Baines
P.E.	4a		A	Ms S. Rai

How to interpret the grades on this sheet:
ATTAINMENT LEVELS as reported in the National Curriculum Sublevels
The nationally expected standard for 14-year-olds at the end of Year 9 is Level 5 and Level 6.
Sublevels are designed to show where the student is within the level.
a indicates that the student is working at the top of the level and is showing signs of moving on
to the next level, e.g. 5a.
b indicates that the student is secure within the level, e.g. 5b.
c indicates that the student has only just started to work within the level, e.g. 5c.

EFFORT GRADES
A – Excellent   **B** – Good   **C** – Satisfactory   **D** – Less than satisfactory   **E** – Little or no effort

CAUSES FOR CONCERN
a – Attendance   **b** – behaviour in class   **c** – general attitude to work   **d** – failure to produce
homework on time   **e** – Not bringing correct equipment to lessons
Where this box is empty there is no cause for concern.

independent thinkers who are able to confidently manage their own learning and as part of this it is quite natural for their behaviour to appear to be rejecting offers of help. (It's so difficult for a parent to be a teacher – even if the parent is actually a teacher!)

At times your child will even resist your best advice – it's all part of being a teenager. (The *Teen Angels* book offers helpful insight and practical advice on the wider teenage issues. See Resources for more information.) Your emotional response may be more than slight irritation but actually their reaction is understandable and quite normal. It's part of growing up and being independent, so see it as a positive thing. Your child might not ask for your help directly, or may turn down your overt offers to help, but he will 'indicate' when he would like assistance with homework from time to time. These indications are much less forthright than you might expect, so you tend to have to read the signs for clues!

Family holidays during term

Wherever possible, take your holidays during school holidays so as to avoid disrupting your child's study by taking him out of school at critical times during his education, such as at the beginning of the academic year. This is especially important if he has changed schools or, more obviously, when he should be taking important tests or exams.

Be open about when you want to take holiday, and check with the school if they will agree to it during term time. The school should carefully consider your request and they may take your child's attendance record into account.

However, be prepared that schools will not agree to your child missing more than a total of 10 school days for family holidays in any one school year, unless there is a very good reason for him to do so. If your child is off school for more than 10 days, the school could set work for him to do while you are away.

Ten tips for supporting your child's study

Your child is going to do better at school if you take an interest in his studies, and even at secondary level there are many things that you can do to help him. Here are some of the most important:

1 Make sure he has a 'quiet space' at home where he can study and revise without the hurly-burly of family life disrupting his studies.

2 Ensure he has bookshelves, desk space and drawers where he can keep his work safe.

3 Get the rest of the family (especially brothers and sisters) to keep the noise down and leave him in peace while he is studying.

4 Make sure he has time to relax and that he gets enough sleep and plenty of healthy food (limit the sugary snacks and junk food).

5 Develop a routine and try to get him to do homework straight away rather than leaving it to the last minute. The 'carrot' is going out with friends; you can negotiate if he wants to organize himself, but he will benefit from a firm steer on routines.

6 Make sure your child tells you what's going on and shows you his school diary or planner (you normally have to sign it anyway). The format of the diary varies from school to school and might include a timetable, KS3 aims, merit pages and also your Home-School Agreement which you would have to sign (see pages 138–41).

7 Some children might benefit from help with a home study plan which is split into, say, half-hour sessions with a break between each one. Perhaps they could tackle the more difficult assignments in the early sessions to get them over and done with.

8 There are useful tests, quizzes and revision guides to be found in bookshops. If you think these might help, get your child to ask his teachers for recommendations.

9 There are a host of 'brain-booster'-type websites offering children interactive learning and revision help for the KS3 tests, so try to find out which ones are the most beneficial.

10 If you have any concerns about your child's progress in any subject then ring the school to speak to the teacher for help and advice.

Times of The School Day

8.30	8.45	Registration
8.45 (8.50 on Mondays)	9.45	Lesson 1
9.45	9.50	Lesson change
9.50	10.50	Lesson 2
10.50	11.10	Break
11.10	12.10	Lesson 3
12.10	13.00	Lunchtime
13.00	14.00	Lesson 4
14.00	14.05	Lesson change
14.05	15.05	Lesson 5

ASSEMBLY DAYS

Tuesday – Years 7 & 10
Wednesday – Years 8 & 11
Thursday – Years 9 & 13
Friday – Year 12

Term Dates

TERM 1

TERM 2

TERM 3

TERM 4

TERM 5

TERM 6

2

School timetable in Study Planner

OCTOBER
(Days in Italian)

ON THIS DAY...
6th Oct 1829

Stephenson's 'Rocket' won the trials to find a locomotive to run on a railway between Liverpool and Manchester.

02 MONDAY lunedì		Due In	Done

03 TUESDAY martedì			

04 WEDNESDAY mercoledì			

Q: In which year was the Football Association formed and what were their original rules?
See: www.11v11.co.uk

Diary page

Home-School Agreement

As a Parent, I will try to

- ❖ Take an active interest in all aspects of my child's school life
- ❖ See that my child attends school regularly, on time and properly equipped
- ❖ Communicate to school all relevant information which may affect my child's work or behaviour
- ❖ Notify the school, the same day if, for any reason, my child cannot attend
- ❖ Encourage my child to follow the school's behaviour policy and support associated action taken by the school
- ❖ Support the school's policy on homework, provide suitable facilities at home, and encourage my child to make the required effort
- ❖ Attend parents' consultation evenings and other meetings at which my presence is requested

Signed _____ Date _____

As a School we will aim to

- ❖ Provide a safe and stimulating environment for your child
- ❖ Ensure that your child fulfils his/her potential as a learner and as a member of the school community
- ❖ Offer a broad and balanced curriculum to students of all abilities
- ❖ Encourage all students to take responsibility for their own actions, feel proud of their achievements and enjoy being a student at the school
- ❖ Keep you informed about your child's progress and general school matters
- ❖ Insist that students observe the school's behaviour and anti-bullying policies
- ❖ Set and mark regular homework, and provide suitable facilities for homework to be researched at school

Signed: *Jim Judson.*   Date: September 2006

As a Student I shall aim to

- ❖ Attend school regularly and on time
- ❖ Bring all the equipment I need every day
- ❖ Follow the school dress code and be tidy in appearance
- ❖ Do all my class work and homework as well as I can
- ❖ Allow teachers to teach and students to learn
- ❖ Eat food in the designated areas and follow the Cherwell code ensuring that all litter goes into the bins
- ❖ Respect the school environment, including books, equipment and other resources

Signed _____ Date _____

6

Home-School Agreement

MERITS

Subject		Subject		Subject		Subject	
Reason		Reason		Reason		Reason	
Signed		Signed		Signed		Signed	
Date		Date		Date		Date	

Subject		Subject		Subject		Subject	
Reason		Reason		Reason		Reason	
Signed		Signed		Signed		Signed	
Date		Date		Date		Date	

Subject		Subject		Subject		Subject	
Reason		Reason		Reason		Reason	
Signed		Signed		Signed		Signed	
Date		Date		Date		Date	

25

Merit page

Last, but not least, never forget to praise your child for his hard work – regardless of how well he does in school tests.

The later years at secondary: choices and options for GCSEs

Choosing GCSE subjects

The next two years of secondary school – Years 10 and 11 – lead inexorably to GCSEs (General Certificate of Secondary Education). Choosing which subjects and qualifications to study in Years 10 and 11 can seem complicated, but it's a hurdle that has to be overcome and your child's choice will not only affect his next two years at school, but also influence which career or college course he follows later on.

Some subjects are so important that everybody has to study them in Years 10 and 11: this is because they cover the essential knowledge and skills that everyone needs for the future.

The compulsory subjects usually taken at GCSE level are:

1 English
2 Maths
3 Information and communication technology (ICT)
4 Science

During Years 10 and 11 there are some other subjects that your child will have to study, but these may not involve any exams or tests; they are:

1 Careers education
2 Citizenship
3 Physical education (PE)
4 Religious education (RE)
5 Sex education
6 Work-related learning

Choosing subjects for Years 10 and 11 and GCSEs

In Year 9 (age 13–14), for the first time, your child will be able to make some choices over the subjects that he would like to study. The subjects that are chosen for Years 10 and 11 (age 14–16) are the ones that will be assessed at the end of Year 11. For most pupils this will be done through GCSEs although, as we show below, sometimes this can be done through other assessments.

The 'Which Way Now?' section on the Connexions website offers a very useful interactive support to help you and your child make choices (see Resources for website address).

Key Stage 4 qualifications

All schools offer GCSEs in a range of subjects, although these may vary from school to school. GCSEs are more academic than vocational qualifications. They involve an emphasis on academic study (researching, analyzing, reading and writing) with some practical work, depending on the subject in question. In general, GCSEs are usually assessed through a mixture of coursework and examinations.

If you don't think your child will benefit from taking GCSEs in all subjects, there are other types of assessments which can be done in addition to the compulsory GCSE subjects.

1 **Short GCSE courses**: count as half a GCSE (they cover half the subject material) and are offered by some schools. For example, your child might opt for a short course in religious studies or PE instead of a full GCSE.

2 **NVQs (National Vocational Qualifications)** are work-related qualifications in business, engineering, health and social care and sport and recreation and are, as their name implies, for those more vocationally than academically inclined.

3 **VRQs (Vocationally Related Qualifications)** are more unit- and module-based, work-related qualifications which are assessed

Changes envisaged for GCSEs

Vocational education versus academic education is one of the main areas of debate in relation to secondary education. One of the latest manifestations of this debate is the government's initiative on new diplomas.

These diplomas will begin in 2008 and will be offered in five areas, from engineering to creative and media. The idea is that partnerships of schools, colleges and training organizations will work with employers to offer applied skills alongside qualifications such as GCSEs, A levels and apprenticeships. Students will be able to learn in different environments, including schools, colleges and the workplace.

Up to 40,000 places will be available for students aged 14–19 for the first new Diplomas in construction and the built environment; engineering; society, health and development; IT and creative and media.

through assignments in subjects such as food hygiene, hospitality and public services.

4 Young Apprenticeships are designed as a taster for the workplace. They combine the normal curriculum at school with two days a week working towards NVQs and up to 50 days over two years gaining experience with an employer, training company or college.

What advice is on offer to help make these decisions?

So, with all these questions and options, this is a time when your child needs guidance in order to make the best decisions he can for impending GCSEs and for his future. This guidance and advice will be offered to him in a number of ways.

Individual Learning Plan

During Year 9 your child should be offered an interview with his form tutor to discuss his subject options and future career plans. Any decisions made at this meeting should be recorded in an Individual Learning Plan (ILP) and he should also receive an options booklet that outlines the subjects that are available to be studied at the school.

An Individual Learning Plan is pretty essential when considering subject options, so make sure that your child has one.

Key Stage 4 options evening

Your school should also invite you and your child to a Key Stage 4 options evening or event, which should provide opportunities to speak to his subject teachers and tutors about the subjects that interest him. At this session it's important that the teacher asks you for your views as a parent: it shouldn't be a one-sided dialogue and you should be prepared to give your input.

It is really worthwhile attending this parent-teacher evening, because it's amazing how little information you will get about school from your child! Again, this is quite normal and is part of his desire to be able to have control over his life.

Narrowing the options

Some children may already have some thoughts about a career, but others may not; after all, life beyond school can seem miles off at that age. Have you discussed the benefits of going to university with your child? Is he aware of this and the other post-school options?

As a rule it's probably best to keep his options open at this stage by suggesting he chooses to study a broad range of subjects, but other factors also need to be considered – for example, does he prefer science experiments to visual art work such as drawing, or is he more comfortable with coursework than exams?

Remember, not everyone has the same learning style.

Coursework is a part of most subjects now, but if you feel your child would do better in exams, look for subjects where more of the assessment is based on exams than coursework.

The big decider: vocational v academic

Perhaps the biggest deciding factor when choosing GCSEs is whether your child is more suited to academic or vocational study. The term 'academic' or 'general' (as in General Certificate of Secondary Education) refers to traditional school subjects, such as English and mathematics, whereas 'vocational' courses tend to promote skills that will be practical for the workplace, such as in engineering or health and social care.

Some children have more strengths in hands-on practical stuff, while others are more suited to theoretical work; both are equally worthwhile. But it has to be said that if your child is going to progress to one of the best universities then it's the academic development that is important.

Helping your child to choose

Your child's school will not be able to cater for every possible permutation of subject choice, as outlined in this chapter, because much will depend on the teachers' expertise at the school and the timetabling of their work, so compromises in the final selection of subjects are inevitable. Ideally, though, your child should do the subjects he enjoys. So you do need, as a parent, to have that conversation with him. You may discover, for example, that he has difficulty separating the teacher from the subject, and because he likes that teacher he'll say 'I like that subject'. This is something that he will need help untangling to decide whether or not he genuinely likes the subject and wishes to continue with it.

Checklist for choices

1 Find out what the options are at your child's school.

2 Which subjects is your child good at? Which ones does he enjoy doing?

3 If he already has a career in mind, are there any subjects he might need to take in order to qualify for it?

4 Choose a broad range of subjects if he does not know what he wants to do after Year 11.

5 Talk to his subject and career teachers.

6 Contact Connexions, a service offering information and advice for young people. There are lots of ways that Connexions can help at the school, online or by phone. A government-sponsored website will advise Year 9 students how to go about choosing their options. (See Resources for website address.)

The chart on page 148 helps you to see the range of qualifications that are possible and their level of difficulty. Notice the way that 'academic' qualifications are mixed with 'vocational' qualifications within levels to emphasize the importance of both.

GCSE revision plans

As your child gets closer to sitting his GCSEs you will need to see an exam timetable so you can work backwards with your child to plan his revision and to agree how much time he will spend on it per day, and so on.

As you help your child build a sensible revision programme you need to talk to him about revision strategies, such as which memory learning techniques might be appropriate and what other revision aids might be needed. Study skills handbooks give

Different levels of qualifications – from secondary school to university

Qualification/ Framework Level	Level indicators	Examples of qualifications at this level
Entry level	Builds a basic level of knowledge, understanding and skills.	Entry 1, Entry 2 and Entry 3, in a range of areas including National Curriculum subjects, life skills, basic skills and skills for working life.
Level 1	Basic knowledge, understanding and skills, and the ability to apply learning to everyday situations.	All GCSE grades D–G, ASDAN Level 1 certificates, basic and key skills Level 1, Vocationally Related Qualification (VRQ) Level 1, for example: OCR Nationals, BTEC Introductory, National Vocational Qualification (NVQ) Level 1.
Level 2	Basic knowledge and/or skills in relation to subject or sector areas; gaining ability to apply learning to a varied range of tasks. This is seen as the minimum level required by employers and is critical to going on to further study and higher level skills.	All GCSE grades A*–C, basic and key skills Level 2, VRQ Level 2, for example: City & Guilds Progression awards, NVQ Level 2, graded examinations in Dance, Speech and Drama.
Level 3	Learning at this level involves obtaining in-depth knowledge, understanding and skills for a higher level of application. Appropriate for people who want to go on to university, or to further training or employment.	All GCSE AS and A levels, Advanced Extension Awards, key skills Level 3, VRQ Level 3, for example: Foundation Diploma in Art and Design, NVQ Level 3, music grades 6, 7 and 8.
Level 4-8	Specialist learning involving higher level of knowledge in a specific occupational role or study. Appropriate for people working or wishing to progress to specialised technical and professional jobs, and/or managing and developing others.	Certificates and Diplomas of Higher Education, Bachelor's degrees, postgraduate qualifications, Foundation degrees, Higher National Certificates and Diplomas, key skills Level 4, NVQ Levels 4 and 5, teaching qualifications stages 1, 2 and 3.

GCSE-specific help and there are plenty of 'revise-wise' style sites, including the BBC's GCSE Bitesize site.

Remember to impress upon your child that the most important thing is the quality of revision done, rather than the amount: revising and studying for exams is all about active thinking, not just passively reading through notes and text books.

So, here are a few things to think about as the big days approach:

1 Find out dates of exams and work backwards.

2 Manage revision time. (That goes for coursework as well as final exams.)

3 Work on memory, for example, with Mind Maps. *The Buzan Study Skills Handbook* offers an excellent aid to home studying. (See Resources.)

4 Consider some collaborative revision with friends – but beware of time-wasting.

5 Use internet revision support.

6 Think about exam techniques such as reading questions carefully; making careful use of time; answering straightforward questions first; understanding that some questions carry higher marks than others.

Although you may be able to offer more direct help with certain subjects that you yourself are confident with and have some knowledge of, it is important that your child is encouraged to become independent and think for himself. You cannot do the work for him.

Dos and don'ts for a child doing coursework

Do get your child to:

1 Plan his project.

2 Choose a topic that interests him, if possible.

3 Find somewhere quiet to work.

4 Research the subject as widely as he can using a range of books and internet information.

5 Ask for help when he thinks he really needs it.

6 Remember the importance of good writtten English in the final product.

7 Stay fresh by taking regular breaks.

Don't let him:

1 Leave projects until the last minute.

2 Think he can write without having researched properly.

3 Go over the word limit.

4 Copy chunks of text from the internet, books or computer programs – it will be obvious to the person marking his work.

5 Watch TV at the same time.

6 Rush things.

Troubleshooting when things go wrong

There is a host of issues that can concern you, as a parent with a child in secondary school, from ADHD, to smoking, to moodiness and to truancy (many of these apply to other stages at school, too). Whatever the issue, get into a dialogue with your child: talking – communication – is the best way to try to solve the problem.

Dos and don'ts for a child preparing for exams
Do get your child to:
1 Make a revision plan and stick to it.
2 Find somewhere quiet to work.
3 Write notes, highlight key areas or record them on tape
– these are all useful ways of revising.
4 Consider memory techniques such as Mind Maps.
5 Work out which revision style is best for him – alone or
with a friend, in the morning or evening, short bursts or long
sessions?

Don't let him:
1 Leave revision until the last minute.
2 Revise for too long at each session.
3 Panic or get flustered. Tell him that if he is feeling anxious
he should breathe slowly and deeply.
4 Rush through the paper. Tell him to read all the instructions
when in the exam and pace himself in answering the questions.
5 Dwell on the exam. As soon as he has finished one, get him
to put it out of his mind and look ahead to the next one.

Discipline

Schools need discipline amongst their pupils if they are going
to be able to teach effectively. In addition to their behaviour
management policies – which cover general discipline – there are
legal requirements on the key issues of:
1 Racial and sexual harassment.
2 Bullying.
3 Attendance, punctuality and truancy.
4 Teachers' use of reasonable force to prevent a child committing a
crime, causing disruption, injury or damage.

Good discipline is based on an agreement between the school and the parents about what is expected of your child. This often features in a signed agreement (the Home-School Agreement, see page 140) and parents are always encouraged to work with the school to try and solve any problems that may arise.

Parents are considered to be committing an offence if they fail to ensure their child's regular attendance at school. If a child is regularly missing school the parents may get a visit from an educational welfare officer. In extreme cases parents can receive penalty notices requiring them to pay between £50 and £100 or face prosecution. However, this is something that is more likely to be resolved through mediation before it gets that far.

Each school's head teacher is responsible for promoting good behaviour and discipline. The head teacher must draw up the school's discipline policy and, by law, she must publicize the discipline policy. She might do this by making it known within the school and to parents, or by bringing it to the attention of students, parents and staff at least once a year.

If your child is behaving badly or flouting the rules at school, his behaviour will be dealt with in a variety of ways, depending on the severity of it and its consequences.

Detention

The dreaded 'D' word can take place during school hours, at lunchtime or even after school. Detention can be given for a variety of reasons, but persistently breaking school rules, poor attendance or lack of punctuality are common ones. If there is a genuine reason for breaking the rules – for instance, because you live well outside the catchment area and public transport timetables mean your child cannot always get in on time – the school should be willing to take this into consideration. However, if, on the other hand, your child fails to attend without a reasonable excuse, the head teacher may decided to mete out a more severe punishment.

Be aware that if your child's detention is arranged to take place outside normal school sessions you are entitled to 24 hours' written notice so you can make arrangements for transport or childcare. The notice should tell you why the detention was given and how long your child will have to stay at school. If your child cannot attend the detention, you should explain why to his teacher or head teacher. She may reconsider the detention in certain circumstances, such as if it falls on an important religious day for your family.

For more serious 'offences' your child might face suspension or exclusion. There are two types of exclusion:

1 Fixed period exclusion

These exclusions are usually for a short period of time and include lunchtime exclusions (what we know as detention). The pupil must return after the exclusion period has expired. In cases of more than a day's exclusion, work should be set and marked. The law allows head teachers to exclude a pupil for up to 45 school days in any school year.

2 Permanent exclusion

This is also known as expulsion and means that the pupil cannot return to the school unless reinstated by the governing body or by an appeal panel.

Peer pressure and bullying

Does your child feel pressure from his peers, for example, to smoke or take drugs or because he thinks it's 'not cool to do well at school'? Peer pressure is a difficult thing to manage: we all take account of what other people think of us, but we also need to be independent.

Parents need to know that such pressures from peers at school do exist. If you feel this is happening to your child, first try to initiate a conversation with him about his relationships and listen carefully to what he says (or doesn't say). This is why communication and, more specifically, asking your child about what's happening at school is so important. (The *Teen Angels* book offers helpful insight and practical advice on wider teenage issues. See Resources.)

Sadly, peer pressure can also take on another, far more unpleasant and alarming guise: bullying. Bullying is a blanket term that includes teasing, calling someone names, threatening or harassment. It can take many shapes and forms – there is even mobile and cyber bullying going on these days. So be aware of it and teach your child to be protective about his mobile phone number, msn access, and so on. Bullying is a big issue for the government, schools and parents and there are various government-sponsored websites which address the problems and provide parental and child support. Visit the DCSF website for an overview of anti-bullying policy and helpful links. (See Resources for website address.)

Truancy sometimes occurs as a result of bullying, and sometimes this bullying can become physical – with the bully taking a child's belongings or even pushing and attacking him. Ignoring and excluding a child from friendship groups is also a form of bullying.

Look out for signs that your child is being bullied, and if you see something you are unhappy about, talk to him about it.

Common signs that your child is being bullied are:

1 He gets upset at the thought of going to school.

2 He claims to feel too 'unwell' to attend school every day.

3 He displays unusual mood swings – becoming very quiet, resentful or more demanding of your time.

4 He has injuries he can't or won't explain.

Tips to help your bullied child

1 Let him know that you are there for him to talk about anything he wants to discuss.

2 Help him to realize that what is happening to him is wrong and help him to build confidence to develop ways of dealing with this situation.

3 Talk together about what you can both do to stop the bullying.

4 Encourage your child to talk to his teacher or form tutor.

5 Contact his form or class teacher directly yourself: she will know all the children well and will be able to help you decide the best way of sorting out the problem.

6 When you talk to one of your child's teachers about bullying, try to remain as calm as you can and expect that action will be taken. The majority of schools will take reports of bullying very seriously indeed.

7 Talk to other parents you feel you can relate to: bullying is rarely an isolated event at school.

If you discover your child is bullying others, don't lash out verbally; instead try to discuss the issue with him and find out what's at the bottom of it. You need to reinforce the idea that bullying is totally unacceptable but that you need to understand the reasons why he is behaving in that way.

Ten tips to help your child at secondary school

1 Create a space at home in which he can do his homework.

2 Include in this a place to keep pens, pencils, calculators and rulers handy.

3 Encourage him to dip into a dictionary to check meanings and spellings.

4 Help him, but don't do his homework for him. If you ask him for explanations it will encourage him to think it through more clearly.

5 Ask if you can read his homework and discuss his progress in each subject.

6 Use everyday activities, such as calculating family finances, to help him put his learning into practice. Show him the kind of things you have to do as part of your work, and as leisure activities, that require different kinds of understanding and knowledge.

7 Plan visits to places where you can go out and enjoy learning together.

8 Watch out for TV programmes and videos that are relevant to his studies.

9 Make sure he is offered a healthy breakfast, such as cereal or toast, before he leaves for school.

10 When you are thinking about buying things for your children, don't forget that books, board games (such as Scrabble®), art materials, and so on, can help their learning.

furthering their education: 16–18

By the age of 16, students are clearly older and more mature than they were pre-GCSEs, but parents take slightly different views about how much independence should be encouraged. Some parents adopt an approach that it is up to their children to take responsibility now they are older, while others assume they will continue to have control over what happens 'while she's living under my roof'. Either way, the information in this chapter is designed to signpost parental support for your child's final years of school learning.

Parental input shouldn't cease once a child reaches the end of Year 11 (usually 16 years old). The main support you offer is likely to be in discussing the sophisticated issues that face your child as the 16-year-old clutching her GCSE certificates moves from 'pupil' to 'student', or faces the major decision: do I stay on at school and continue education, or do I start work? If she does decide to continue her education, now is the time that you need to be on hand to guide her and to discuss with her the options of AS and A levels, and later the possibility of higher education qualifications.

Continuing with education: what to study?

If your child decides to take A levels, or other qualifications, then she will have to select which subjects she wants to study for the next two years. To encourage her to do this, get her to ask herself two simple questions:

1 What are you good at?
2 What do you enjoy doing?

Discuss in detail the positives of each response, then weed out the negatives and anything your child has doubts about. Most students do better when they study a subject they like, so that should be a key factor in determining how you steer the discussion with her

A word on work

Of course, many teenagers won't want to go on to Sixth Form, university or anywhere else for further education. Legally a child can leave school and start work at the age of 16 (depending on the date on which her birthday falls). However, it is generally agreed that higher education offers many benefits to young people – beyond just obtaining the qualification of a degree. The government is so convinced about these benefits that for some time it has been attempting to raise university participation to 50 per cent of young people. So this option should be considered carefully and not rejected without thought. If leaving education and moving into a career is your child's preferred option, there is one key thing you should take into consideration: make sure that whatever your 16-year-old chooses to do, it will provide her with training and nationally recognized qualifications, or at the very least some kind of continuing learning opportunity. If your teenager does go into work, make sure she realizes that it does not preclude her from seeking further qualifications in the future.

about choosing subjects. Her decision should not just be made on the basis of what she *might* need to further a possible career; too many people get hung up on choosing the right A levels purely for a particular career.

Having said that, some careers do require qualifications in particular subjects, so you need to investigate that now to make sure that she is not closing doors on potential careers by dropping certain subjects. For example, if your child has her heart set on a medical or veterinary career, biology A level is important.

However, most teenagers don't know what they want to do, so if this is the case with your child (and as this book is about getting the best for your child at school), encourage her to think about how she can broaden her learning horizons for the next two years in continuing education.

Choices for further education

The next step in your child's education will be quite different from what has gone before – even if she is carrying on in the sixth form of her secondary school, a familiar setting, that often includes friends and teachers she already knows.

The sixth form stage offers a way of learning that involves more coursework and more personal time management; uniforms are more relaxed or possibly not even required and generally your child will be treated more like an adult.

Where can she study?

Students can choose from four key types of further education establishments:

1 School sixth form
2 Sixth Form college
3 Further Education college
4 Specialist college

Each type of institution has its own structure and atmosphere and will offer a different range of subjects and courses.

School sixth form

Your child may be able to continue her study at her own school's sixth form, or the sixth form of another school. Sixth forms feel quite different from the rest of, say, a larger, mixed 11–16 comprehensive school that they might be attached to. Sixth forms offer a different range of subjects and learning options from those your child has previously been used to, and they offer a more adult learning style than in Year 11.

Sixth forms vary a lot in size, but they will all offer AS level subjects in the first year, moving on to full A levels (called A2) in the second year. Some schools will also have arrangements with other local schools or colleges to give you a wider choice of subjects and qualifications, especially with work-orientated qualifications such as BTECs, NVQs and Key Skills (see pages 171–72).

Sixth Form colleges

These colleges offer similar courses to school sixth forms, but the key difference between them is that Sixth Form colleges focus only on education at this level, and they also tend to be larger than school sixth forms.

Further Education Colleges

Further Education colleges can offer similar courses to Sixth Form colleges and, like sixth forms, they also vary a lot in size and in the subjects and facilities they offer. One key difference here is age: fellow students may include adults of all ages as well as young people. These establishments also tend to offer more vocational and work-related courses.

Specialist colleges

As their name suggests, these further education colleges specialize in certain subject areas – such as art and design, agriculture and horticulture, dance and drama – as well as offering 'special needs' courses and support. As these colleges are not so commonly found, your child may have to travel some distance to get there and might even need to live on site during term time. If this is the case she could qualify for financial help. However, some courses are only available to people over the age of 18.

What your child needs to get in

The entry requirements for admission to this level of education are quite complicated because they differ according to the type of institution that your child is applying to – even Sixth Form colleges located in the same geographical area can have different requirements.

You need to look carefully at the website or prospectus of every institution you are considering applying to in order to be sure about the detail, but in general you should expect the following requirements:

a Students within the geographical area will be offered places before those outside the area.

b A good reference from the school where GCSEs and equivalents were studied is essential.

c A successful interview at the Sixth Form college.

d Appropriate grades at GCSE, particularly for the subjects the child intends to continue to study.

In general, the minimum entry requirement for a Sixth Form is often having five grade Cs or above at GCSE, and an average GCSE point score of 40 in the best 8 GCSE results (see chart below). A grade 'B' or above is often recommended in all subjects being taken to A level.

GCSE Grade	Points Awarded	GCSE Grade	Points Awarded
A*	58	E	28
A	52	F	22
B	46	G	16
C	40	U	0
D	34		

Students who are entitled to extra time in exams, have Educational Psychologist assessments or special educational needs, should indicate this on their application form. This will not affect their application, but it will help the school provide for their needs should they be offered a place.

Helping your child to choose

1 Get a prospectus All schools and colleges publish their prospectus as a free booklet and, more likely these days, a downloadable online PDF. This prospectus will describe the facilities and the courses on offer and also the qualifications needed for admission. You can search for school and college websites by keying in the school's name or searching via the directgov search engine. (See Resources for website addresses.)

2 Locate the Ofsted report As with all the other stages of education outlined in this book, the first port of call for information on a school's achievement and attainment, and its contact details, is the Ofsted report for your preferred choice. Remember to check the sections of the report about the subject departments that your child is interested in.

3 Go to open days Nothing beats a personal visit to find out what a school or college is really like – even if it is your current school sixth form. That's why it's vital to go to any open day or evening that you are notified about; it is an opportunity to see the facilities and meet the staff and some of the prospective students.

4 Review the exam scores of the subject department you are interested in.

Where to get advice

You can get advice to help you decide on where and what to study from your:

1 current teachers

2 parents/carers

3 friends/relatives

4 Connexions personal adviser at school. You can also speak to a Connexions Direct adviser for free, confidential advice (see Resources for contact information).

5 School and college websites

Applying for a school or college

When it comes to the time to act on your decision (students start applying for popular or specialist courses in the autumn term of Year 11 and usually for other courses in the spring), your child can apply to more than one Sixth Form or college. Many colleges offer online applications through their website, or they will send an application form on request.

Your child might well have quite strong views about what next stage is best for her: whether it is on to further academic study or perhaps a more work-orientated qualification. Hopefully you will be able to have quite sophisticated discussions with her about this and you can encourage her to take a strong interest in the information that's out there and to use it to help her make her own decision as to what she will do next.

However, the decision will also be influenced by more mundane matters, such as the location of the college and the ease of access to it by public transport (say goodbye to school buses). If the college is further away than your child's current school, the safety and cost of the route to the new school could be an important consideration. If you are hoping that your child might pass her driving test at age 17 and know she will have access to a car, parking can also be an issue.

Qualifications

There are broadly two main types of qualification on offer for the first year of the sixth form (Year 12):

1 Academic (traditional school subjects in AS and A level and the International Baccalaureate).

2 Vocational (these are work-related. There's a whole raft of them, including NVQs, BTECs, City & Guilds, OCR, Key Skills and Apprenticeships).

Academic

The predominant academic qualifications at this age are AS (Advanced Subsidiary) and A (Advanced) levels. The focus of these is to study particular subjects in depth – there are over 80 to choose from. Most students studying for A levels take three or four AS levels in their first year, although some take five or six.

AS levels prepare the ground for those subjects a student wants to continue with at A level. However, some subjects will be completed only at AS level and not taken further. Doing a range of subjects means students keep their options open over which ones to study as a full A level. Most people choose three subects to continue studying at A level but some do four or more. A levels normally take two years to complete as full-time study in school or college.

Universities will grant admission chiefly on the basis of A level and AS level results, so most people use AS and A levels as a lever to go into higher education. Good A-level results can mean access to undergraduate studies at some of the best higher education learning institutions in the world – but they are also useful if you want to go straight into certain jobs.

University entry

Normally, to take a higher education course your child will need at least two full A levels or the equivalent. If she is applying to university or college, A levels earn the following points in the UCAS point system:

Grade	A level	AS level
A	120	60
B	100	50
C	80	40
D	60	30
E	40	20

(UCAS – University and Colleges Admissions Service – is the central organization that processes applications for full-time undergraduate courses at UK universities and colleges.)

AS levels

In the first year of Sixth Form your child will be working towards her AS levels. These qualifications are effectively considered to be half an A level in terms of 'value' – for instance in terms of the university admissions process, where scores are relevant to decisions made about which students to take.

So the AS level can be viewed either as a free-standing qualification, or as the first half of the full A level. At the end of the AS year, your child has two options (depending on the preference of her school or college): to take the AS level qualification only or continue into the second year and go for the full A level.

A level

In the second year of the sixth form (Year 13), your child will complete the full A levels (called the A2). This is not a separate qualification, but rather the second half of the A level. The subjects your child studied at AS level in the first year are now narrowed down to three for A-level study.

The AS and the A2 qualifications are usually assessed on a mixture of 70 per cent written exams and 30 per cent coursework, including the assessment of practical skills in some subjects, such as the sciences or art. A levels are required to assess general knowledge of the whole subject in addition to specific areas studied in detail.

Making the grades

AS and A levels are graded A–E (A being the top mark), and the results are announced in August and March each year. If an exam doesn't go well, don't panic: your child may be eligible for special consideration, so speak to the teachers as soon as possible. It is possible to re-sit units that are part of the AS levels. Once students are happy that they have done their best, the grades are 'cashed in' with the exam board. The school or college can also ask for a re-mark or recount, but the school will incur a cost for doing this, so it is up to them to decide if there is a reasonably strong case. (Usually they will only do this for pupils who have significantly underperformed in relation to their expected grades.)

International Baccalaureate

Another qualification on the radar these days is the European-wide International Baccalaureate (IB), which is taken by students aged 16 to 19. British schools are beginning to adopt the IB, although there is a continuing debate about whether it prepares students more suitably for future study than A levels.

Its chief selling point is that it's a single qualification rather than separate qualifications for individual subjects. Assessment is done mainly through exams (marked externally), but in nearly all subjects teachers mark individual pieces of coursework. The Diploma normally takes two years to complete, with exams taking place in May and November. Results are based on points rather than grades, with 24 needed to obtain a full diploma.

Baccalaureates do now officially count towards the UCAS point system (see page 168) needed to get a place in higher education. An IB Diploma total of 24 points will earn 280 UCAS points – the same as two 'Bs' and a 'C' grade at A level. The maximum of 45 points will earn 768 UCAS points – equivalent to more than 6 A levels at grade 'A'.

Vocational

However, A levels and Baccalaureates are not the only qualifications that have value: if your child enjoys learning practical skills, or knows what job she wants to do in the future, she may want to opt for for the vocational, work-related qualifications that focus more on practical, rather than theoretical, learning. These include NVQs (National Vocational Qualifications), BTEC National Diplomas and Certificates, GCSEs in applied subjects, City & Guilds and OCR Nationals – to name a few key ones.

These qualifications are another educational world in their own right, and trying to understand how they work can feel like learning a new language. However, the key question remains: will your child benefit more from theoretical research-based learning or from hands-on, career-orientated skills?

See Chapter 5 (page 144) for a note about the new diplomas that the government is introducing (and the directgov website for more detailed information).

NVQ

This stands for National Vocational Qualification and involves work-related tasks designed to help develop the skills and knowledge necessary to do a job effectively. The outcome is a recognized qualification that is related to a particular industry or sector. NVQs can be studied at work, college or as part of an Apprenticeship and include key job markets such as business and management; sales, marketing and distribution; healthcare; food, catering and leisure services; construction and property manufacturing and production and engineering. They can be a means to an end in themselves, or they can be used as a springboard for taking higher education courses in a related vocational area, such as a Higher National Certificate, a Higher National Diploma or a Foundation Degree.

BTECs

BTECs are wide-ranging and well established – from engineering to e-business, via travel and tourism, they offer learners a more practical approach to subjects that are available at GCSE and A level. They can be combined with other qualifications, most commonly key skills, but also with AS and A levels.

City & Guilds

City & Guilds offer 500 qualifications in 28 industry areas; from health and social care to hospitality and catering. School-dinner hero Jamie Oliver and F-worded chef Gordon Ramsay have both benefited from these, as have fashion retailer-designer Karen Millen and the ubiquitous post-renaissance man, Alan Titchmarsh.

OCR Nationals

OCR Nationals are more practical, work-related qualifications that give learners an insight into a particular vocational area: from Health and Social Care to IT in Public Services, also Sports Science.

Vocational A levels

Just to blur things a bit, there is also a range of 'Vocational A levels' available (also called 'GCEs in applied subjects'). There are 10 subjects to choose from which offer a broad introduction to a vocational area such as business or tourism or design. (Colleges tend to offer a wider range of vocational courses than schools.) Like A levels, they are taken over 2 years and can be studied alongside other qualifications such as AS levels and NVQs.

Skills-based qualifications

Other qualifications, called Key Skills, cover the basic reading, writing and working with numbers skills that employers look for in employees and which show them that the job candidates can work with others.

What to consider in the debate over continuing education

1 What is your child good at, and what does she enjoy?

2 Does your child want to learn something new? For many courses, she may not need any previous experience.

3 Does the course structure suit her – does she prefer end-of-year exams, continual assessment or a mixture of both?

4 Will the learning style suit her – is she better with classroom discussions and/or practical workshops?

5 Where will the course take her – does it fit in with her long-term plans?

6 Does your child prefer a practical approach to learning? Has she considered a work-based training option, such as an apprenticeship?

Preparing for AS and A level exams

The same ground rules apply at this stage of your child's education as for preparing for any exams – particularly with regard to ensuring exam dates are written in the calendar and encouraging and monitoring her revision timetable. However, parental input is also likely to feature in more concentrated fits and starts when she asks for help with coursework.

Home study leave

Firstly, be prepared for the fact that before GCSEs and AS and A level exams your son or daughter suddenly seems to be coming home during the school day when you thought she should be at school. Well, the fact is that Year 12 and 13 students will be given some private study time during the school day.

The length and duration of these home study sessions depend on the school (and some don't give this type of leave) and they are unsupervised. This can be a mixed blessing. For many children, having the opportunity to live 'like a student' rather than a school pupil is liberating and, if your child is pretty motivated and well-organized, it can mean an effective use of time. In fact, most students do use the time productively, but it is a long period in which they do not have any contact with their teachers.

It is also true that some young people might find that their study leave becomes 'computer-gaming leave'. If both parents are out at work during the day then it could be a lonely and undisciplined time for the child; those with a parent at home at least have the benefit of wake-up calls, coffee and meal breaks, and the opportunity to talk through their stresses.

So, to help your child get the most out of her home study leave, it's vital for you, as parents, to ask her:

1 How long the study leave is.
2 What revision timetable she is planning during that leave.
3 What subjects, modules or topics are involved.

4 How you can help. (Extra art supplies? Special trips to museums, galleries, hiring DVDs, libraries? And so on.)

Selecting a university

How good is a university, and how do we know if it is any good? These are just some of the many factors that come into play when you are helping your child decide which university to apply for, and here are a few more that are worth considering:

1 Qualifications needed and selection process – Some universities have stringent entry requirements.

2 Location – How convenient or accessible is the university? Does your child want to be 40, or 400, miles away from home? Is a rural campus environment preferable to spread out city-centre locations?

3 Facilities – In what condition are the lecture theatres, study rooms, libraries, and so on? How easy are they to get to and from?

4 Amenities – Take a look at the canteen, café, sports field and car parking.

5 Reputation – Has this department got a name for being a leading establishment in the subject your child wants to study?

6 League tables and audit ranking – Most parents will be aware of the national newspapers' league tables before they come across more sophisticated information. For example, *The Times* and *The Guardian* newspapers each have university league tables. One major difference between these two is that *The Times* guide weights research heavily, whereas *The Guardian* one is more concerned with teaching. This single fact resulted in Cambridge being top of one table and Oxford the other in 2005. You can see from *The Guardian*'s criteria for their university league table below that all is not as simple as it might appear at first.

7 Quality of teaching – A body called the Quality Assurance Agency looks after formal evaluations of university teaching – not research, though, which is covered by the Research Assessment Exercise (see page 177). It's similar to Ofsted but with one vital difference – universities are assessed against the aims they set for themselves, which means that they retain control over their teaching. During an assessment, a team of people will visit university departments to read

The Guardian criteria

The tables are based on data for full-time undergraduates; we haven't yet cracked the more complex task of measuring part-time students, so distinguished institutions such as the Open University and Birkbeck College do not appear. One day, perhaps.

We have rated courses against the following criteria:

○ Teaching quality, as rated by graduates of the course

○ Feedback, as rated by graduates of the course

○ Spending per student

○ Staff/student ratio

○ Job prospects

○ Value added – comparing students' degree results with their entry qualifications

○ Entry score

From these we have compiled an average for each institution, weighted by numbers of students and mix of subjects.

TAKEN FROM: GUARDIAN NEWSPAPER UNIVERSITY GUIDE - HTTP://EDUCATION. GUARDIAN.CO.UK/UNIVERSITYGUIDE2008/0,,2027789,00.HTML

When you look carefully at the ways in which the data are collected for league tables, you'll find that there are always limitations in the information. In addition to the limitations of the way data are compiled, there are also basic gaps in the data – for example, music technology is not covered in the tables as a separate degree subject but it is instead categorized under music (the academic study of music is quite different from the study of music technology or other practical aspects of music).

Just because a university is regarded as better than many others does not necessarily mean it will be the best for your child. Some universities offer specialized courses that others do not. Also, universities have many departments, all of which will have different strengths and weaknesses. There are often strong departments in what are regarded as less good universities, and there can be weak departments in good universities.

through documentation provided by the university, to interview staff, and to observe some teaching. It would not be feasible to assess a whole university in one go, so a selection of subjects, groups and their courses are chosen. If you want in-depth information about particular teaching in university departments you can view these reports at the QAA website, or if you think that students' views of their institutions are the most relevant indicator then try the national student survey of teaching quality (see Resources for website addresses).

8 Quality of research – There is some debate about the extent to which it matters to a prospective undergraduate if academic staff are 'research active' and are good researchers. If students are strongly interested in the academic side of study then this element does matter, because they may well go on to study for PhDs and Masters qualifications and for that level of study well-qualified staff are essential. There is no simple correlation between best research and best teaching though, and the best universities get both right. Our view is that the quality of research in a university *is* important. The Research Assessment Exercise (RAE) is carried out every five years or so to assess the quality of research (not teaching) in university departments. This leads to some kind of scoring of the quality of research. Most university websites will have a link to their research pages, and a reference to the RAE score will be made if they were successful.

9 Suitability of courses on offer for your child – Is the course *exactly* what she wants to study?

10 Accommodation – What is the condition of the rooms and amenities on offer? Are they on site or spread around the town? How much do they cost (this can vary quite a bit across the country) and do you pay in holiday time? Are they mixed? Is there a campus shop, laundry, and so on?

11 Student social life – Does the student union bar look fun, or is there easy access to a buzzy student social life elsewhere?

Five steps to securing a university place
1 Apply for a place

Applications for university can be submitted from mid-September in the year before students go to university. This means that finding out about universities and all that they offer needs to be done at the very latest in that autumn term, and some of it, ideally, before that. Help for parents and students in relation to the application process can be seen at the UCAS website (see Resources for website address).

2 Go for an interview and/or open day visit

Each university or college has its own application procedure. Some may ask you to come for an interview and bring a sample of work, or you may be asked to take a test. Others will offer you a place based on the information on your application and the minimum requirements of certain A level criteria. If you do receive an offer from somewhere you've not visited, attending an open day is absolutely essential to help you decide whether or not you want to study there.

3 Apply for financial help

In 2007/2008 new full-time higher education students studying in England could be charged up to £3,070 a year in tuition fees. As well as fees, students (and their parents) have to pay for day-to-day living expenses such as accommodation, food, books, travel, and so on.

Once the UCAS application has been made, students can apply for financial help: they don't need to wait for an offer. Student finance is a vast area that is outside the remit of this book, but this is the time to start researching the crucial area of Student Loans to cover fees and living costs (which need not be repaid until the course has been completed and your child is earning over £15,000 per year) and the Maintenance Grant, which is non-repayable if the applicant has a disability, children of their own or adult dependants. (See Resources for the NUS website which will give more guidance on living costs.)

4 Get a confirmed offer

Offers will either be conditional (dependent on getting certain grades on your current course) or unconditional (you automatically get a place). You can make one firm choice and one insurance choice (to keep as a back-up option). You should hear either way by the end of March, although for popular courses you may not hear until May.

5 If you don't get an offer

If you don't get an offer, or you don't get the required grades, you can go through the clearing system, whereby universities and colleges advertise course vacancies. Tens of thousands of students find places this way.

Open-day checklist for choosing a university

The following checklist will help you and your child get real 'gut-feel' feedback on each establishment – giving the complete picture which reading a prospectus, scanning a league table, or navigating the dedicated website cannot do.

1 Did the course tutor explain the nature of the course and how it would run over the three years? Did he explain the rationale/driving force behind the course and what was expected of the students? Or did he perhaps reveal how or why his course was tailormade to the subject and how it 'crossed over' with other subjects/modules/facilities? What were the post-graduate opportunities like? Did they have a secondment/workplace relationship with local businesses?

2 What extra-curricular opportunities are available? For example, music, sport, societies, and so on.

3 Was the 'housekeeping' and management of the open day professional, welcoming and as publicized?

4 Did they hand out literature about the university, such as on the courses, accommodation, Student Union or the finances and costs?

5 If a portfolio of work was asked for, was this used? Was there a one-to-one interview?

6 What was the welcoming speech by the Dean or Head of Department like?

7 Did the university staff take the visitors around the facilities? What were they like?

8 How was the overall demeanour and presentation of the staff?

9 If current students were involved, what were their views of the course?

10 Did the visit include a tour of the accommodation?

11 What was your overall impression? Were all your questions answered?

Above all, such a visit should provide a superb 'snapshot' of the university and the degree course on offer on its own terms, and for comparison with the competing university open days. If your child is serious about a particular university and the course offered, then an Open Day visit is a must.

So, we have taken you and your child from nursery to university in 181 pages and there are some key messages from this book which, if heeded, will really support your child on her educational journey.

✪ Increase your understanding of the education system – by reading this book you are already a long way forward.

✪ Talk to your child as often as you can about how her learning is going.

✪ Have the confidence to go and talk to the people who are educating your child: praise them for the good (and sometimes almost miraculous) work they do; listen carefully to what they have to say; give them more information about your child so they are better able to help her; challenge them strongly but constructively if you think they are not serving your child well.

And, after you've done all of this, don't forget that politicians have huge influence over how schools carry out their work. Education is not only vital to you and your child – and fascinating as a subject in its own right – but it is also something that you pay a lot of money for with your taxes! As a tax-payer and voter, use your influence to change things in the best interests of all children, as well as your own.

Resources

There are a host of government, commercial and charity organizations that offer advice and resources, from baby-age provision to bullying helplines. Some have excellent learning downloads; others contain reports specific to certain schools. Here is a selection of useful, 'first port of call', parent-friendly sites. Do bear in mind, though, that websites do change their url, even government ones, or pass their 'sell-by' date.

BBC
http://www.bbc.co.uk/schools

Does what it says on the tin – gives a good level of advisory information broken down into early years, 4–11, 11–16 and 16+ and is a learning resource for both home and schools. Again, this is divided into early years, primary, secondary and 16+, with extra help on citizenship and plenty of advice on revision. The BBC learning section is more focused on adult learning and skills, but it does also have good links to children's learning sites and core subject sites. It includes a special parents' section as well as a revision guide, educational games and safe chat room.

Connexions Direct
www.connexions-direct.com/whichwaynow.
Free helpline: 080 800 13 2 19

An exceptionally helpful and not condescending 'what-to-do-with-your-life/education' site for 13–19-year-olds. Connexions Direct offers practical and relevant information and advice for secondary school children on how to make learning and career decisions and includes links to health, money, housing, relationships, travel, rights, bullying and disability. It also features a step-by-step guide to Years 10 and 11, with regard to choosing the right subjects, career, action plans.

DCSF (Department for Children, Schools and Families)
http://www.dcsf.gov.uk
Tel: 0870 000 2288 (DCFS HQ)
This site provides government-sponsored, multi-faceted and easy-to-navigate support for parents on how to help their child with their learning; including advice on choosing a school and finding childcare. The Department for Children, Schools and Families (formerly the Department for Education and Skills) also produces achievement and attainment tables that show how well schools do in exams and tests and gives the latest information on government educational initiatives.

Teachernet is a handy website with a parent's centre which has advice on bullying and many other subjects dealing with children's education and they publish a useful guide for parents: www.teachernet.gov.uk/wholeschool/sen/parentcarers/

Directgov
www.direct.gov.uk/en/EducationAndLearning/index.htm
The first, and probably the best, one-stop search for most of the issues about their child's learning that are likely to concern parents. This site contains clear-cut, government-sponsored guidance which is laid out under several large banners: including early years learning, schools, life and options for 14–19-year-olds and university and higher education. It is particularly helpful when looking for schools in your area, and trying to decide on the right one for your child because it includes links to Ofsted reports and curriculum requirements and explains the required qualifications (www.direct.gov.uk/en/EducationAndLearning/Schools/

ChoosingASchool or www.direct.gov.uk/en/EducationAndLearning/
QualificationsExplained).

It also includes good links to other educational websites, to related
topics such as health and student finance and to other issues
relevant to young people.

EYFS (Early Years Foundation Stage)
http://www.standards.dfes.gov.uk/eyfs/

This website provides information about the curriculum that is
covered in early years education – from birth to five. It also includes
video clips which show examples of teaching and learning in the
different areas of the curriculum.

Homework research

There are too many websites that are helpful sources of information
to assist with homework and projects to list each one, but don't
forget your local library as a first port of call. Remember, too, that
once you join you will also be eligible for free online access via the
library's/local authority website to such subscription-only sites as
Britannica Online and Oxford Reference Online Premium – both
are excellent and authoritative references for homework
and projects.

National curriculum online
http://www.nc.uk.net

For every subject, this site explains what needs to be studied,
including guidelines, attainment targets and notes and
links to online teaching resources. The site is run by the
Qualifications and Curriculum Authority (QCA). Or you can try
http://www.direct.gov.uk/en/EducationAndLearning/Schools/
ExamsTestsAndTheCurriculum, which is a directgov site that is
related to National Curriculum teacher assessments and Key
Stage tests.

need2know

http://www.need2know.co.uk/learning

This is a student/teenage-orientated lifestyle site with plenty of stuff on sexual health, smoking and bullying, but it also covers learning, homework, revision coursework, qualifications and good links to other useful sites.

Ofsted

www.ofsted.gov.uk

Tel: 08456 404045

A must-visit site when choosing your child's learning provision options – at any age. A parent and carer's shortcut shows you how they inspect, explains why you should read the report and offers a portal to the latest inspectors' reports via postcode or school's unique reference number – from nursery to sixth form colleges.

ParentMail

https://www.parentmail.co.uk

ParentMail is an e-note delivery service from school to parent that is designed to bypass those 'notes-at-the-bottom-of-the-school-bag' scenarios. Schools subscribe to the service and are responsible for the content of the messages and determine which message groups will receive them. Parents register to be recipients of the relevant message groups.

Parents online

http://www.parents.org.uk

Tel: 01489 559110

While this site sells useful materials and does feature commercially-sponsored competitions, it also provides useful insights into a wide range of topics that are appropriate for parents of primary school children – from child obesity to crib sheets.

Raising kids

www.raisingkids.co.uk

Tel: 0208 883 8621

This website addresses commonly felt worries by parents, such as the internet and parenting skills, and also includes a helpful education timeline and general overviews and advice on education.

Sure Start

http://www.surestart.gov.uk

Tel: 0870 000 2288

Sure Start is the government programme that brings together early education, childcare, health and family support. It includes a special section for parents entitled 'Birth to Three Matters Framework' which concentrates (as the name suggests) on the early years stage of a child's development. The programme aims to roll out a network of up to 3,500 children's centres for young children and their families, making sure that the most disadvantaged areas will all have access to at least one.

    The philosophy behind its work is based on the Every Child Matters programme (http://www.everychildmatters.gov.uk) which, again, has a parents' guidance section.

24-hour museum

http://www.24hourmuseum.org.uk

Tel: 01273 623266

An excellent guide to museums across the UK for parents who want to stimulate their child's curiosity and offer them alternative help with topic work. It has a teacher and children hit but no parent 'hit' as such; however, the whole site is a treasure trove of living learning with educational and Key Stage-linked resources.

Special education needs

The British Dyslexia Association

http://www.bdadyslexia.org.uk

Helpline: 0118 966 8271

The British Dyslexia Association influences government and other institutions and aims to promote a dyslexia-friendly society. If you think your child might have dyslexia, http://www.dldcn.com allows you to check if your three-and-a-half to six-and-a-half-year-old is showing signs of dyslexia.

Dyspraxia Foundation

http://www.dyspraxiafoundation.org.uk

This website is run by a UK charity and is a resource for parents, and teenagers who have the condition, and also for professionals who help them.

University websites

Each university will have its own website whose quality and navigability can be a useful indication of what the university may be like as a 'real' rather than 'virtual' establishment.

Aim Higher

http://www.aimhigher.ac.uk/Uni4me/home

Although based in northwest England, this site offers UK-wide links and answers to all your student queries about getting into university and what it all means.

NUS (National Union of Students)

http://www.nusonline.co.uk

The National Union of Students website offers all essential information for students, including advice on educational and emotional issues as well as guidance on university funding and student rights.

QAA (Quality Assurance Agency)

http://www.qaa.ac.uk/reviews

Tel: 01452 557000

The Quality Assurance Agency is an independent body that reports and reviews higher education establishments.

TQi (Teaching Quality Information)

http://www1.tqi.ac.uk/sites/tqi/start

The Teaching Quality Information website gives access to up-to-date information about the quality of higher education in UK universities and colleges. The site is supported by the Government and the National Union of Students.

UCAS (Universities and Colleges Admissions Service)
http://www.ucas.com
Tel: 0870 1122211

The Universities and Colleges Admissions Service is a central organization responsible for managing applications to higher education courses, and 'clearing' which matches students without offers to courses still available each September/October. The UCAS website also includes a cost of living budget calculator at http://www.ucas.com/studentfinance/costs/cost.html

Reading list

Buzan Study Skills Handbook, Tony Buzan (BBC Active)
Little Angels, Dr Tanya Byron & Sacha Baveystock (BBC Active)
Teen Angels, Dr Stephen Briers & Sacha Baveystock (BBC Active)
How to Help Your Child Read and Write, Dr Dominic Wyse
(Prentice Hall Life)

Acknowledgements